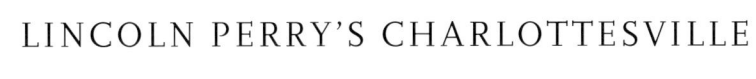

LINCOLN PERRY'S CHARLOTTESVILLE

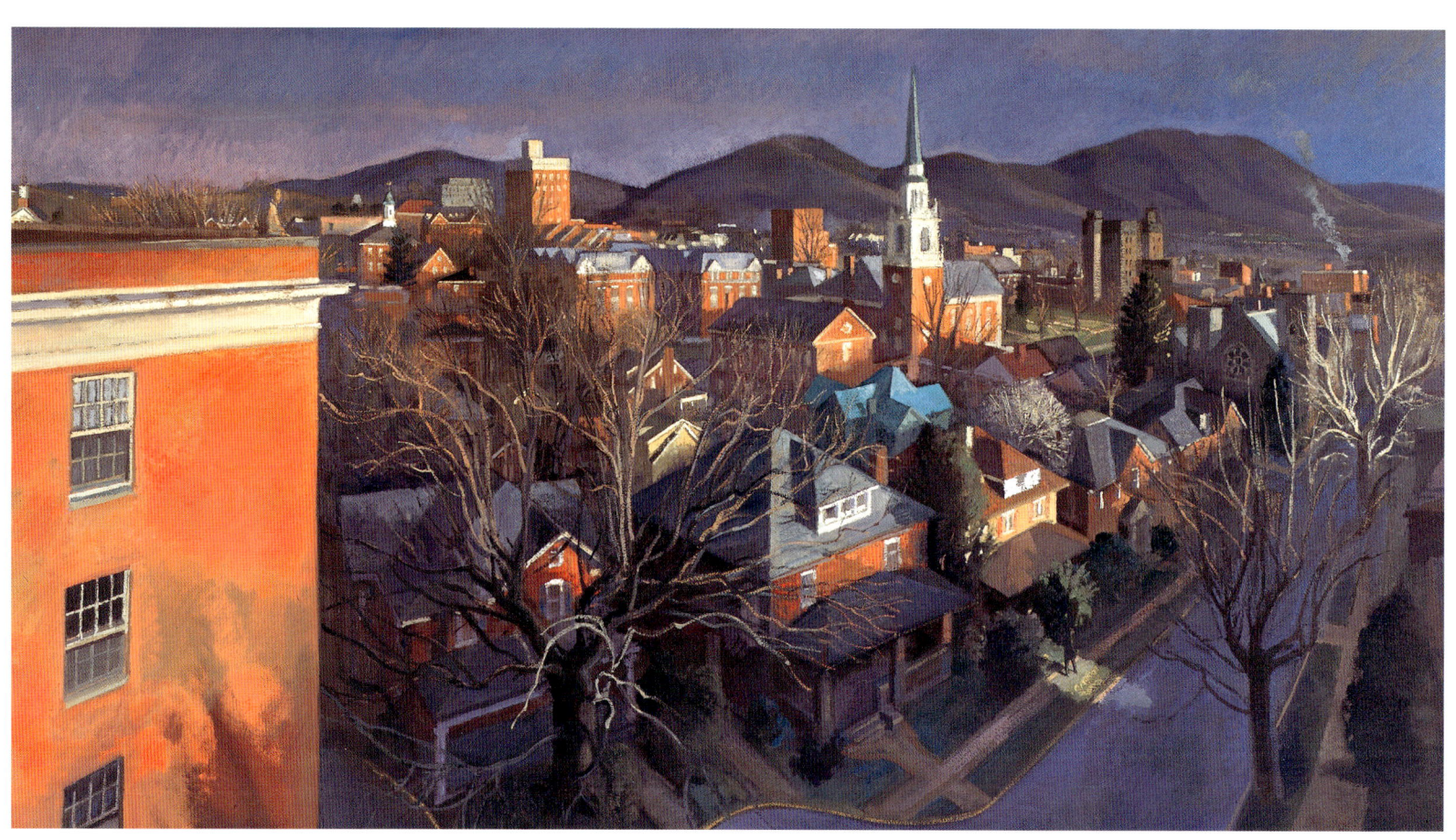

LINCOLN PERRY'S CHARLOTTESVILLE

Paintings by Lincoln Perry

With an essay and interview by Ann Beattie

UNIVERSITY OF VIRGINIA PRESS   CHARLOTTESVILLE AND LONDON

Publication of this volume was assisted by a grant from the W. L. Lyons Brown Jr. Charitable Foundation.

University of Virginia Press
© 2005 by the Rector and Visitors of the
University of Virginia
All rights reserved
Printed in China on acid-free paper

First published 2005

9 8 7 6 5 4 3 2 1

Library of Congress Cataloging-in-Publication Data
Perry, Lincoln Frederick, 1949–
    Lincoln Perry's Charlottesville / paintings by Lincoln
Perry ; with an essay and interview by Ann Beattie.
        p.   cm.
ISBN 0-8139-2503-7 (cloth : alk. paper)—ISBN 0-8139-2504-5
(cloth, limited edition : alk. paper)
    1. Perry, Lincoln Frederick, 1949—Themes, motives.
2. Charlottesville (Va.)—In art. I. Beattie, Ann. II. Title.
ND237.P376A4 2005
759.13—dc22
                                            2005014979

Contents

Acknowledgments

This book reflects work done over a period of twenty years, including four on the Cabell Hall mural, and so there are many to thank. I am grateful to all those who made the Cabell Hall commission possible. Ruth and Bob Cross and Don and Alison Innes had not only the idea for the mural but the drive and generosity to help see it through to completion. Their energy was complemented by the support of Lee Brown and his W. L. Lyons Brown Jr. Charitable Foundation. I was glad to see the mural dedicated to John Casteen, and very gratified by his reaction to the final work.

I would also like to thank those who made this book possible, including, once again, Ruth Cross and her daughter, Prue Brown, and son-in-law, Paul Stetzer, who thought the project might be feasible and worthwhile. And again the W. L. Lyons Brown Jr. Charitable Foundation, and Cary Brown in particular, were extremely generous, while Lyn Bolen Rushton of Les Yeux du Monde Gallery and Mark Saunders of the University of Virginia Press have offered help that has been invaluable.

Many thanks to Tom Cogill for his superb photography, and to those kind enough to make work available for him and others to photograph, sometimes in remote locations: Robert Carroll, Jane Haslem, Mary Lee Settle, Ruth Cross, Don and Alison Innes, Monica Gibson, Carol Stevenson, and Betsy and John Casteen.

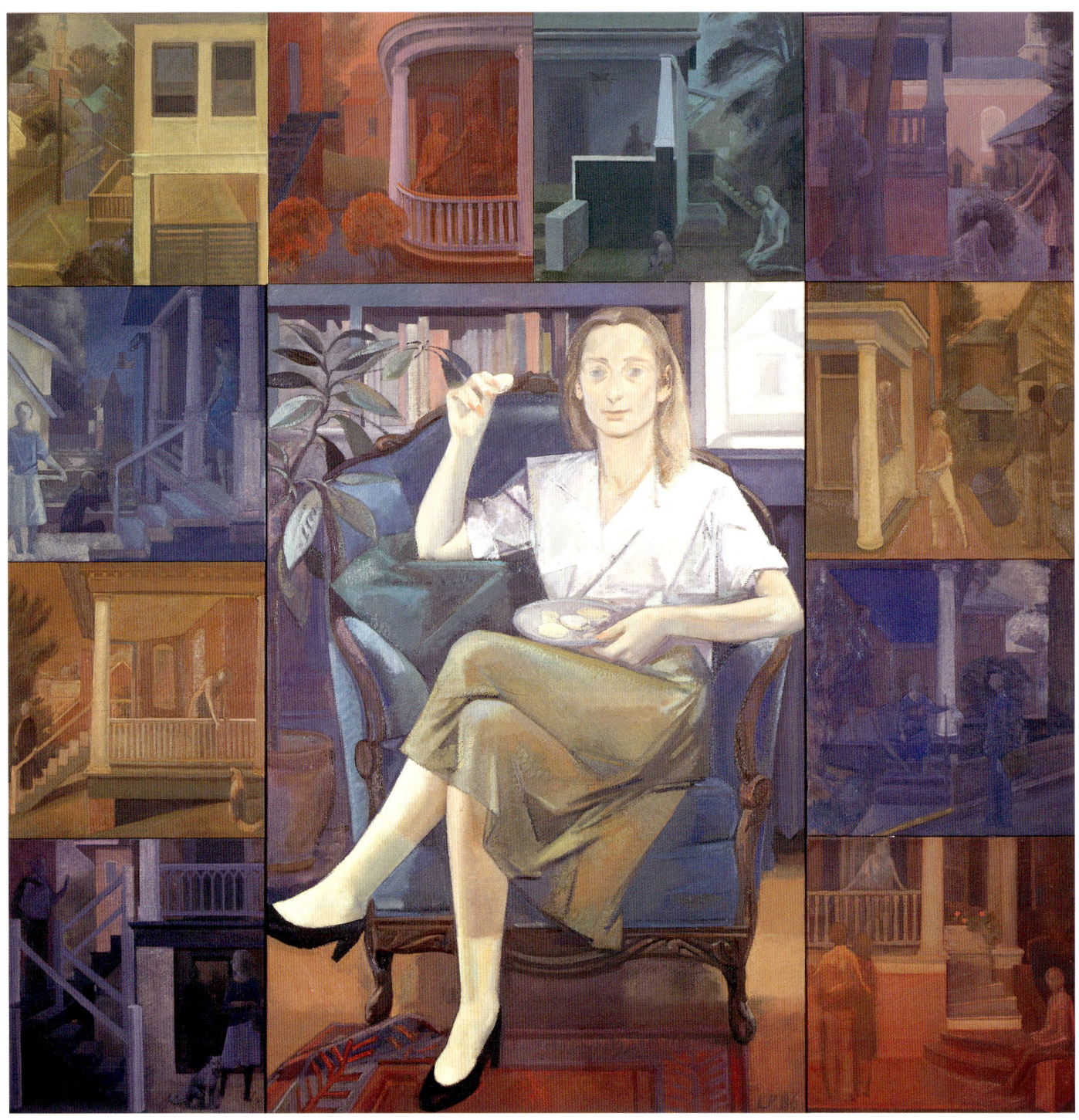

PLACING LINCOLN   *by Ann Beattie*

In transient America, we are fascinated by place. We are inundated with special issues of magazines devoted to peoples' memories of the places where they grew up, the places they love above all others. Place has been deified, and with deification come certain expectations: we must travel to more and more remote spots; we must move forward, yet cast our Gatsbyesque eye backward. Our vacations must be adventures, our contexts global.

What does all this have to do with Lincoln Perry and his paintings of Charlottesville, Virginia? The place both disturbs and calls to him: it's a paradoxically comfortable and uncomfortable not-quite-home he has been drawn to many times for reasons he can't easily articulate. He visited Charlottesville as a young man (hitchhiking to visit a girlfriend), later lived in Charlottesville for ten years, left, and recently returned to buy a house—though he also lives elsewhere and, when he can, goes to Europe to paint. Although from time to time he has taught art at the University of Virginia, he has primarily been a self-employed painter with the luxury of being able to choose where to live. He has a wanderlust that his wife (me) considers impressive. I suspect that if Charlottesville had Italy's trees and Key West's cemetery, he might spend even more time in town.

For Lincoln, no individual place has proved perfect—either for living or for painting—but when he's in town he goes out into it, repeatedly, to observe the way it changes in different seasons, or as one day elapses. On a day when a windstorm takes down a big tree on the university grounds, he pays homage as if he's attending a friend's funeral. He might know the fate of more former bushes and trees than anyone but a landscape architect, and still mourns one particular tree that provided U.Va.'s Lawn with its only deviation from the vertical. (See page 3.)

Inevitably, as he has returned to the town during different periods of his life, he's reapproached it with changes in his own way of looking at things, and with different interests in structuring and executing paintings. He loves many things about Charlottesville, and it has served as a constant, though ever-changing, source of inspiration to someone I would not describe as a person who likes small towns, or who even prefers the United States to Europe. He could go (he does go) elsewhere. But in self-inflicted rootless times, it's a place that has retained special, personal associations: family who attended the university; our meeting; good friends; his interest in history; his love of Jefferson's architecture.

Pleasant associations and a degree of comfort are always suspect, and at best only part of the story. Artists are also motivated by discomfort, and intrigued by contradictions and complexity. If there's nothing to wrestle with, there's little depth of involvement. As anyone who lives in Charlottesville knows, the place is something of an oddity: a Democratic bubble in a Republican state; distinct groups of people (the writers; the horse people) who don't often mix. I think that Lincoln likes the town's quirkiness and its lack of uniformity. It's also a place that allows him to practice the x-ray vision so many visual people have for underpinnings: the contradictions that can be drawn upon and aesthetically dramatized; a painter's sensitivity to light, but also to sound, to growth, to loss. Obviously, some of the paintings are in a major, others in a minor key. Perhaps I'm projecting, but it occurs to me that Lincoln may be interested not so much in the much-discussed loveliness of Charlottesville as he is in its being a place he hasn't quite settled on, a place he lives in part-time that's always eluding him: in a strange way—I feel this way, at least—it's impersonal enough to project upon, and therefore possible to love. It's almost approachable, yet not. Try taking a walk in the county, and realize that you have to walk on the shoulder as trucks fly past, and that all the land is fenced. Yet other times—the most unexpected times—the Lawn at the university can be inexplicably empty, and the moon can look a certain way, and the smell of the ground, and of the magnolias, can be sweetly pungent.

The place sparks his imagination, and with his paintbrush, he sparks it, charging the air with a bit of unexpected—but very recognizable—light. People make much of light in paintings, and fair enough: so do painters. To someone who doesn't paint, however, the light might seem particular, yet be taken for granted. It takes someone like Lincoln, who notices the way it drifts and casts shadows that have a blue or a violet hue unlike other shadows, to make a viewer realize that in part *because of* the light, he or she can identify the location. For whatever reasons, he's willing to be vulnerable to the place: a conduit for its changes, its disjunctions, its sometimes unexpectedly lovely coherence.

Just as realist painters must know the fugitive, elusive nature of reality and the level of artifice inherent in their project, painters of place are aware that their subject—in this case, Charlottesville, Virginia—has an uncontained life of its own. The unparaphrasable is what artists tend to trust, so while it's often physically beautiful and diverse, the town isn't inherently provocative or confrontational, like Las Vegas, or mind-bogglingly spectacular like the California coastline heading toward Monterey.

There is also the much-talked-about spirit of Mr. Jefferson, a presence so strong it can't be ignored. We must philosophically accommodate to an apparently inevitable expansion, while the place has continued to resonate with the ideas and ideals of the man who once looked down on it from his mountaintop. People want the land because they want privacy. They want the downtown mall (in Charlottesville, an outdoor, pedestrian-friendly zone) because they want to be part of the public parade.

People have endless good and bad ideas about the place—but almost always they assume it needs to be changed. (Well, *of course* the asbestos has to be removed. And who objects to a good wine store?) As is happening all over the nation, people are moving back downtown, buying condominiums, having their morning coffees. (There's still the lunch place where the workmen eat; you can buy bread anytime you get sick of your croissants, the argument goes.)

Though it seems rather unlikely to me, knowing that Lincoln doesn't easily filter out urban sprawl, or even members of the opposite political party, he seems endlessly able to find a personal walkway through the scaffolding and bulldozed streets and buildings in medias res to connect with the place and to tacitly acknowledge the timelessness of some of Jefferson's best thoughts and to reconsider them as they are woven into a contemporary context. There are always the implicit questions about change: How much is too much? Is this going to work? What does it mean when a certain history pervades a place, but in a layered and disjunctive way (a subject of Lincoln's paintings of mostly bewildered tourists surveying the ruins of the Roman Forum)? When I think about it, third-millennium Charlottesville exists as a daily enactment of Lincoln's internal debates about how to paint and how to live, apparently almost synonymous concerns.

At this point, a note to the reader. This is being written by a writer who distrusts narrative, about a figurative painter of narratives who often says he

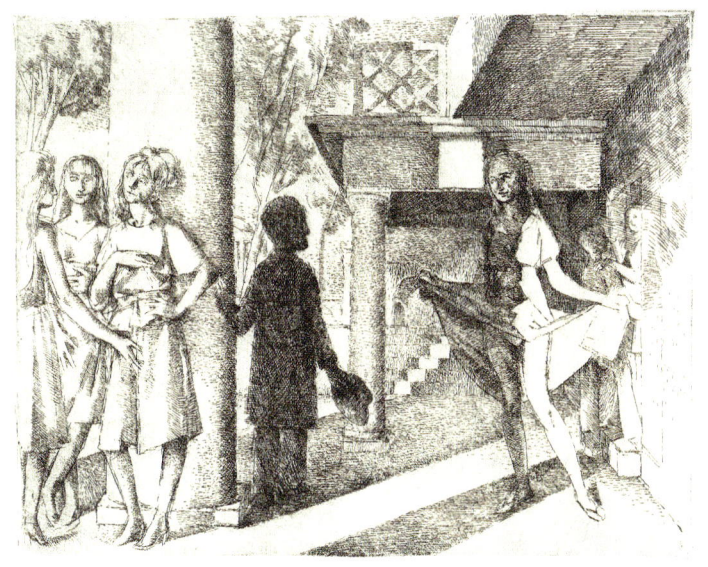

has no idea what people do. I mention this not to make you think us peculiar and deficient, but because so many introductions seem to suggest that artists know what they're doing: that they are gifted (whatever that means), and that they have a will to express themselves, and do so. I'm skeptical about how true this is, but I'll avoid sweeping generalizations and confine my remarks to myself and to Lincoln.

When the viewer looks at Lincoln's paintings, he or she may be immediately drawn to them, though it takes a while for things to sort themselves out. On first quick glance—the advantage, but also the liability, of things visual—the viewer is usually able to see, in a general sort of way, what is there. But more often than not, Lincoln offers an octoscope instead of binoculars to assist in our viewing: multiple panels have a confusing, sometimes static, sometimes overwhelming, contradictory complexity that puts the viewer on sensory overload, and then —just when you think your eye is moving quickly enough, and that your brain might catch up—the shapes shift, and your perception skitters to reveal another mesmerizing shape: you try to look at it in its entirety, yet you can't, because you can't trust it not to move—especially because it's painted so as to keep the eye in motion. So perhaps you squint, to take in only an aspect of the painting, or, if it has multipanels, the primary panel, on top, or the one that seems particularly involving, on the left . . . Eventually more is revealed, which is not to say that there are not continuing complexities and ambiguities.

Lincoln is true to his sensibility. He paints not so much out of a sense of defining things but rather to reveal that there are always multiple possibilities: there are the steps to one of the pavilions seen frontally, and there are the same steps seen from the side, obscured by a bush. As someone who majored in history as an undergraduate at Columbia and who began to understand for the first time that so-called historical facts had much to do with who was presenting those facts and why, and as someone who has a proclivity toward encompassing different viewpoints and resisting the idea of a representative (or inevitable) narrative, Lincoln finds multiple perspectives to be not merely an interesting diversion but a presentation of the artist's thoughts and feelings as he wrestles with unexpected moments of beauty, disharmony, or unexpected ironic juxtapositions. Clarity is not always trustworthy or even inviting; those who understand

Robert Frost's "Stopping by Woods on a Snowy Evening" comprehend that even the poet wouldn't think the museum stairs less traveled by made all the difference. When Lincoln's eye takes different perspectives, you are obliged to do the same. Things shift, just as they do in life.

It's a standing joke in our house that "there are three possibilities." Even when Lincoln says there are two possibilities, there end up being three. It makes things more interesting—at least to him, because it's true to his way of looking at life— though the multiple-possibilities game can get a little maddening in terms of what restaurant we go to for dinner. It also suggests that possibilities, themselves, are real exactly because they are multiple, and that they need to be given their say; in his paintings, it's as if he personifies possibilities as figures. Mythical underpinnings are often used to suggest shared subliminal meaning or subtle continuity; there are homages to other painters, sometimes invoked to complicate, as well as to clarify; even fond in-jokes: just what you'd expect of someone who has studied the history of art but who also has humility and an unusual sense of humor.

What artists don't often say is that it's the amusement factor that keeps them going through the rough parts. In my work, a minor character, allowed in one quick quip to compromise the other characters I've so painstakingly created, is always welcome. Autonomous, unmanageable characters give me the courage to trudge on. Your little antagonists have to be in the work, whether they're the airborne kite that won't stay still long enough to paint or characters who have clearly slipped out of your grasp. Whatever is being created—in order not to be hermetically sealed by its own artfulness—needs breathing room. The problem is how to suggest that it's there without diverting too much time and energy into invoking it, so that it doesn't distract the viewer or reader. In Lincoln's painting the history of art is real and present, and an allusion to another painter is more a collaboration of kindred spirits than an homage or an appropriation.

Lincoln is a figurative painter, at home with abstract thinking and painting. What we see becomes form and color and proportion—and yes: the painting also remains a depiction of steps you can ascend or descend. He's fond of quoting Corot and Bonnard to the effect that it all comes down to light. In viewing his work over time, or the work of any painter who creates a world, the cumulative effect is that it's instructional, and that when you begin to consider things in their own terms—to follow their lead—you've taken an important step toward silencing the self-referential chatter in your head: the story you tell yourself about what's good, what's bad, what's expected and what's not.

In a book Lincoln likes very much, *Out of Sheer Rage* by Geoff Dyer, the author presents an account of his failure to write his book because his subject eludes him, and this struggle results in a very funny book. There is a passage about the writer's envy of artists that I find extremely informative. Dyer writes:

> Writers always envy artists, would trade places with them in a moment if they could. The painter's life

seems less ascetic, less monkish, less hunched. Instead of the austere mess of the desk there is the chaos of the studio: dirty coffee cups, paint-smudged cassette decks, drawings of the artist's girlfriend, naked, on the walls. . . . For the painter work means a more intense physical engagement in life, it begins with carpentry (making stretchers) and ends in glazing, varnishing and framing. Even though it thereby involves labor the painter's work—or so it seems to the writer—never seems like work. In the age of the computer the writer's office or study will increasingly resemble the customer service desk of an ailing small business. The artist's studio, though, is still what it has always been: an erotic space.

Well! Surely he speaks the truth, and the wonderful messiness is much more romantic than wads of paper thrown in a trash can. The painter is *in there,* doing something, touching something. (This envy has turned many writers into good cooks, by the way.)

On the rare occasions when he's painting indoors in Key West, I sometimes watch Lincoln out of the corner of my eye, and less frequently I wander into his space and sit backward on a rickety orange office chair donated by his mother. (I never, ever see Lincoln sitting in this paint-smeared chair; nevertheless, it serves as an obstacle to everyone: our approximation of an old, slumbering family dog.) With phone on the table, Bob Dylan revival in full Whoooooooooooooah, Lincoln stands, cocking his head, barefoot, war paint on forehead or tip of nose, paintbrush at his side pointing down, like a conductor who has decided the musicians can

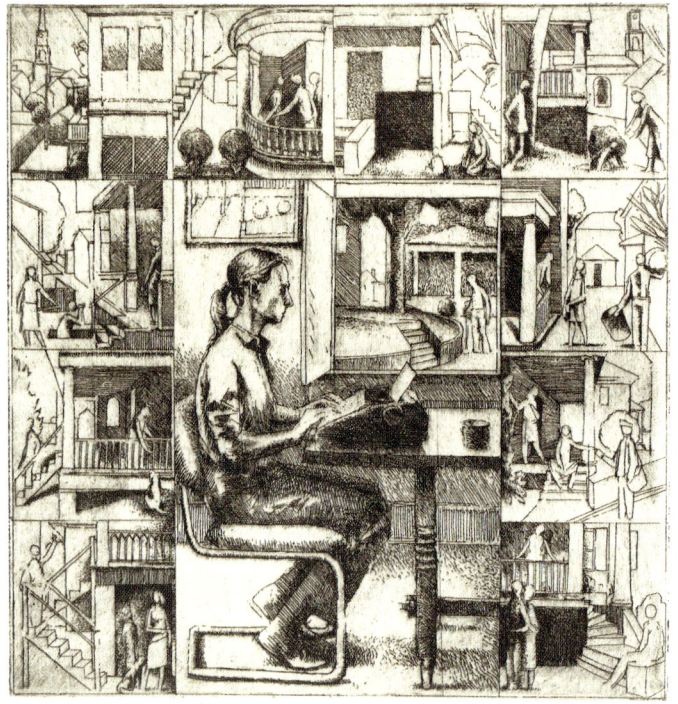

sees part of the writerly equivalent of the body-in progress—a sentence instead of a hand, or even a word, instead of a finger—the rest of the body will evaporate and I will be left with nothing. In a way, I feel that I'm writing by holding my breath, as if thereby withholding breath from my character, because it needs a life of its own that must transcend what I'm creating, or there will be no finished story. If someone sees it—including me—it will disappear. But Lincoln . . . moving forward, singing along with song lyrics, squinting—all of it is his enviable, odd little dance (always, always accompanied by music, whether playing loudly in the room or—you, too, can save your marriage—through headphones) that's physically interactive with his dancing partner, the painting.

Writing, I sit as silently as possible, not making a move, to better encourage or trick the character into coming out of hiding. But this is not Lincoln's method, at all. (Come to think of it, we both work in the same way we converse: he has questions; I rarely do; he likes to get something going; I like to see what unfolds.) As I understand it, the visitor is part of the painting, as is the sound track, the art book open on the floor to a painting by Poussin or de Kooning; the phone call that comes in is part of the painting, interrupting the already interrupted momentum, thereby shaking up ideas.

When he's painting, Lincoln knows—the lucky artist gets to know, because he can touch it if he wants—that his subject matter is not going to die on him or recede into mist or in any other way cease to exist. He might paint things out, but that's another matter. If he is in the process of painting a

figure the rest of it out themselves. Once he's ascertained that I don't have yet another computer problem he has to solve, he'll continue to squint and to endlessly approach and back up from a canvas hung from a somewhat expandable masonite wall that blocks the entrance into the kitchen.

I not only look at what he's painting but notice with envy that Lincoln can paint almost anywhere, including the landing into our small, many-windowed Florida apartment. Visitors usually don't faze him, whereas I do a body block of my computer screen if someone walks in while I'm writing, no different than if I were hiding a fugitive. My fear (wait'll you hear this one) is that if someone

figure with an opaque, featureless orb on top of its neck, he can tell you which vegetable he wishes you'd buy at the store, or where he thinks the checkbook is. I am completely amazed by this, and it transcends my awe for all the reasons Geoff Dyer remarked upon; I'm jealous because he can let you look right at the mystery and still continue to perform magic. And furthermore, he doesn't think of it as magic—which is not to say that it's easy (you should see the sketches and preliminary marks); it might be insufficient, or problematic, or disappointing in any number of ways, but it won't cease to exist unless he decides some or all of it doesn't belong, whereas most writers will tell you—really—that their characters are capable of putting on their hats, leaving the room, slamming the door, and never returning, even if no one but the writer is their audience. No: Lincoln's creations are indelibly there in the faint marks of charcoal; they get clearer and clearer (if they're meant to), they are adjusted and repainted and removed and perhaps put elsewhere, but they're there because they live in his understanding of them.

But what are they doing? Beautifully choreographed, they might be lovers or prisoners in a road gang. And what is the story? People come up to me at openings and ask me to explain what's going on in some of his paintings. "That's our kitchen," I sometimes say dully, knowing that the answer is as insufficient as it is banal. They're not about something, they are something: prisoners are seen taking positions in a dance. In depicting them this way, Lincoln has also taken a position: he has revealed his sensibility, his assumptions about finding beauty in unlikely places. In conversations with viewers of Lincoln's paintings I resist trying to come up with answers because I don't want to know the story. I'm drawn to the narrative precisely because I don't know it and because, by its very nature of being a painting, it has to be a different story from any story that could be put into words. If it could be told to me—paraphrased, in effect—there would be no need for the painting. (No inherent virtue in things remaining ambiguous: just a reminder that ambiguity does not exist merely to be figured out.)

When we first met, I was surprised and embarrassed when Lincoln would ask other couples, "What do you do during the day?" and "Do you talk to each other?" I thought the implication was that we did nothing of consequence and that we didn't talk to each other. Now I suspect he was covertly asking for an insufficient answer, because of course people weren't going to rattle on about doing their taxes or getting the oil changed, or express their feelings about their child's first-grade teacher. I think *Don't tell me; fail me* was what Lincoln really wanted, in spite of the ingenuous question. Because he's not an illustrator. He paints because he doesn't know, and ultimately doesn't want to know, what the story is. The story is the painting: they're synonymous, symbiotic, though neither precludes the other.

We're often drawn to Lincoln's unusual perspective, I think, because he gives things the mask of informality, and we trust that in the same way an imperfect, unposed snapshot can be more telling than a formal portrait, or when an aside is more revealing than the lecture. In fiction, a tape recorder is useless in capturing how we process speech; people are used to tuning out what's said to them, to filling in other peoples' sentences. They paraphrase stories in their own minds, approximate, and express ideas as clichés, which makes "real" speech seem unnatural. Without seeing the people talking, we miss the cadences that announce seriousness or the lack of it, the gestures that undercut words. Narrative painting, itself a fiction, involves such subtextual subterfuges; we are like visitors who don't speak the language struggling to comprehend, thrown back on intuition to make sense of native behavior. The viewer must do some work, but must also have faith that the painting converses with itself with considerable intelligibility. Painters don't capture the moment, as is often said as a form of approval: they take real liberties with chronological time and do it so convincingly that you don't question the odd (and impossible) stopping of time.

Both the Cabell Hall murals and the *Music of Time* series are about one of Lincoln's constant concerns. Simply put: the passage of time. In this case, for a student at the University of Virginia—through the seasons, with various achievements and mishaps, in symphony with others and then alone, the student matriculates and goes into the world. The rhythms and repetitions of time can be seen as a dance, though less reassuring images can intrude, as when the arrow of linear time is pulled down to Earth by gravity. Time and overpopulation are Lincoln's preoccupation; count the figures in the Cabell murals. We all live vicariously in our creations, but

I think painting the Cabell murals was an ideal challenge for Lincoln because while he had to project himself into the main figure's position and mind, he was more familiar with being on the other side, so to speak: he'd been a teacher at a place where he had not been a student; he loved Jefferson's initial concept of the university, yet had misgivings about the ways in which the university meant to expand (and also about the building his mural would be installed in: its creation cut off the view of the mountains beyond, blunting an important element of Jefferson's vision). It was a chance, then, not just to have his own dream but to honor the dream of Jefferson, by illusionistically painting the panels as if the building were transparent.

As you might expect, a lot of research and planning went into the painting—this from a painter whose total immersion in planning involves, early on, the banishment of certain ghosts of ideas. Flannery O'Connor said about writing, "You have to put it there before you can take it away." It seems obvious, but it isn't—that you can't think through something or paint something in your mind: you have to physically do it, because the hand will instruct you. Artists will tell you this is true (perhaps more so the more accomplished one becomes: then, who believes in shortcuts?). The painting went through significant rethinking, and then of course it also asserted its own will. This is all I can figure out about why Lincoln selected a redhead to be the model of the young woman, then was dismayed about the colors a redhead couldn't wear (debatable, having seen the maquette in which she wears red). The paintings are large, and as he

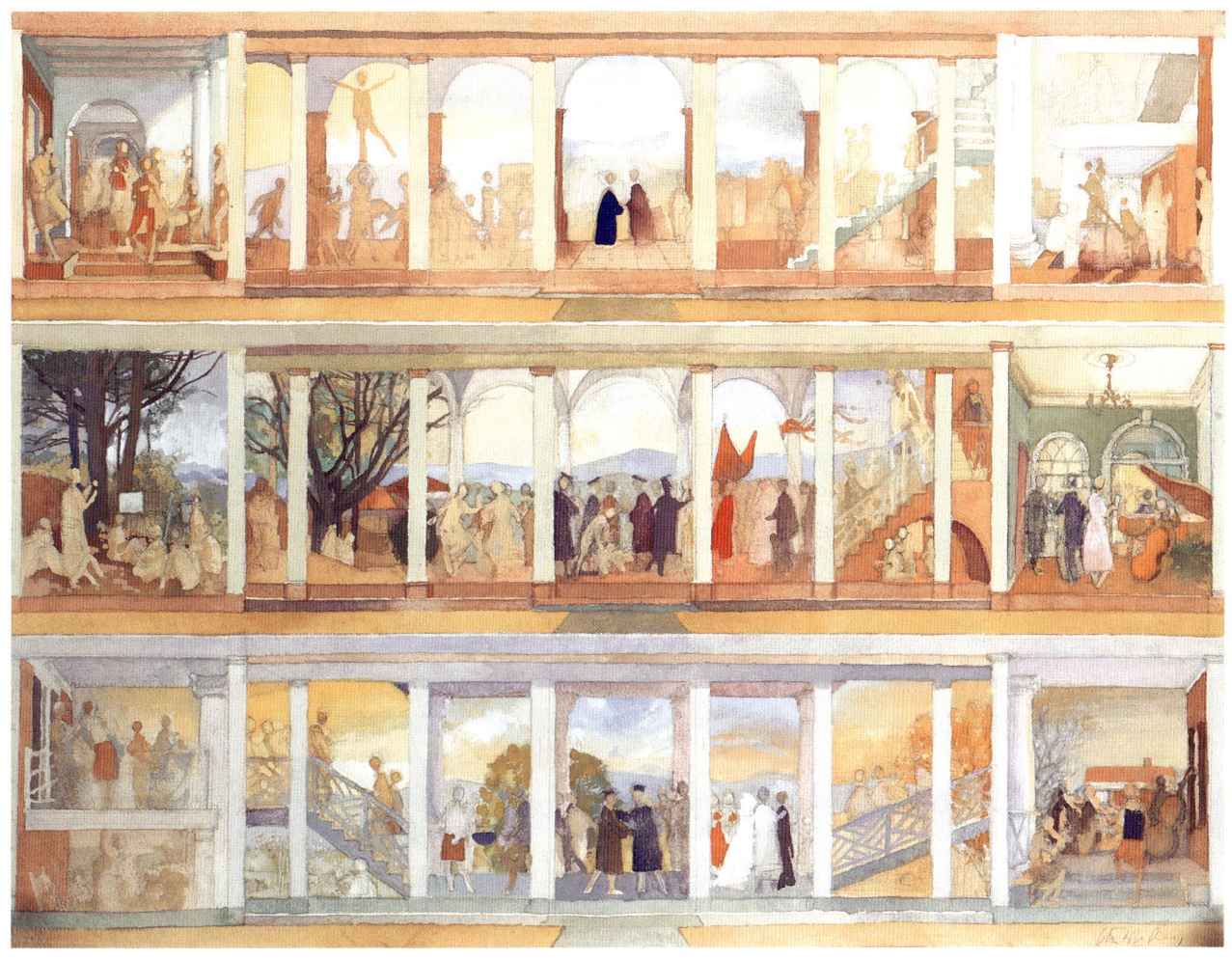

worked, there was initially no way to see them together. Even individual paintings were so large that part of the canvas would be rolled as he worked on the rest. He could not work in Cabell Hall itself, for obvious reasons. He worked from measurements he made there, took notes on how the light came in at different times of day, figured out what other light would be needed to augment it, and finally even amused himself by adding a faux shadow beneath a figure's feet, on the real baseboard, after the panels were installed.

When people ask me to make an analogy between painting and writing, I want to say that they are not at all alike, and the day I have to maneuver the pages of a novel out my office window, I'll play the analogy game. Did he envy the clean compact-

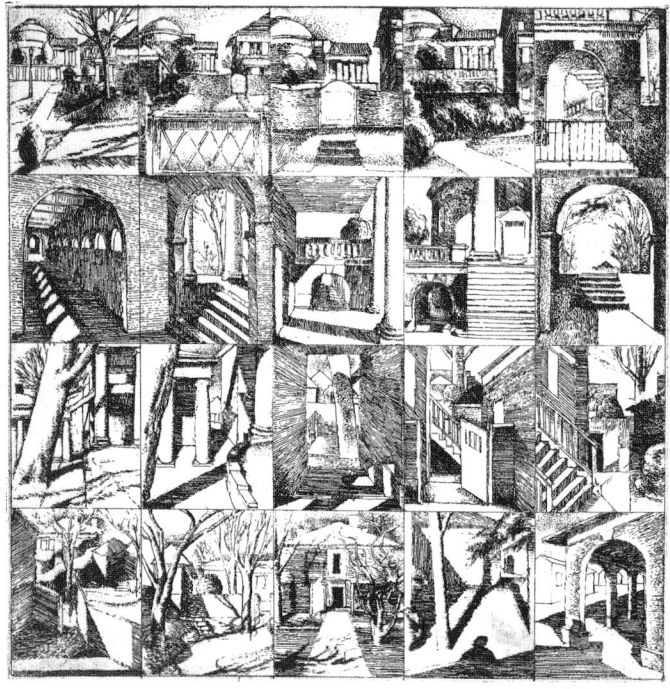

stant adjustments, problems of perspective, unanticipated difficulties (anyone knows this who has tried to make even an omelet). It's all an illusion, created with paint. As stories are just constructs of words.

V. S. Pritchett has written, "Because the short story has to be succinct and has to suggest things that have been 'left out,' are, in fact, there all the time, the art calls for a mingling of the skills of the rapid reporter or traveler with an eye for incident and an ear for real speech, the instincts of the poet and ballad-maker, and the sonnet writer's concealed discipline of form." So, too, with painting: what has been left out—almost the entire world, really—has to be suggested, so the painting will convince. It has to transcend its borders, extend beyond the frame, be a contained entity that lets you know that, paradoxically, it is uncontainable. It is the painter's or the author's responsibility to let the viewer or reader know that they are aware of what's been omitted, and that the omissions, as well as the negative spaces, count for as much, if not more, than what's there. The fifth panel in *Music of Time XX*, on pages 62–63, shows us a bride at her wedding; the serpentine wall, practical and metaphoric in Jefferson's design, becomes symbolic, suggesting a serpent in Adam and Eve's garden. The curving pattern continues throughout, with the back of the chair the woman sits in, with the suggestion of a half circle made by the wedding gown's uplifted train.

Though the panel of the woman sitting in a chair is not exactly a non sequitur, it functions similarly; it appears as a random view of someone who turns

ness of my process from keyboard to publisher as he wrestled his rolled-up canvases, twelve feet long, out the attic window in Maine, then drove them to Charlottesville, where they were unrolled, put on the floor, cut (hold your breath), the wall painted with wet glue, the canvas rolled onto the wall (yes, with a nerve-wracking mismeasurement on the installer's part), with elements of some panels matched to the next? Most likely.

Without spontaneity, the paintings couldn't exist. Their energetic moment of conception can't disappear in their execution. Preplanned as they are, of course they don't emerge as planned: there are con-

out not to be a major character, and as such, even in retrospect, it's so unexpected a depiction as to be almost out of time and place (context). I could invent a story, but why? The figure reminds us that there are other, private narratives going on while the painting sequence is itself building toward a private narrative that becomes public: a wedding. Yet the wedding isn't the expected culmination. This is a painting by Lincoln, after all. The geometry with which he began—the somewhat simplified, almost reverential recording of shapes —is returned to in the enigmatic final panel. Wedding over, the gate is open, and a shadowy figure, who no doubt has a story of his or her own, is passing by.

It would be an oversimplification to say that shape and form, abstraction, and architecture are triumphant, yet not unrealistic to say that amid the mysterious players of this story, they express coherence and a concrete reality: a kind of certainty we can't identify in the events. In conversation, non sequiturs are surprisingly indicative of a speaker's train of thought, even though the speaker may not realize what he or she has revealed. In writing and painting, though, the artist places things deliberately: there can only be the fiction that something is a non sequitur when it's selected. Lincoln's unexpected inclusions—his interruptions of the trajectory; his mysteriously presented figures—function as non sequiturs, though they are really intentional. They suggest that the story must be, or at least might be, much more complex. Once interrupted, the viewer has to rethink the story he or she had been putting together consciously and subconsciously. The lack of exact transitions, the inclusion of what might be called minor characters, the lack of specificity in figures, along with the near personification of nature, force the viewers not only to participate in creating the story but to simultaneously realize their inability to do so with any certainty. It's insidious, but fun: a sort of secret wink that collusion is required between artist and viewer, but also the tacit admission that the creator and the perceiver share a vulnerability. How, exactly, do you give the viewer or the reader the secret wink? In part, by being quick on your feet: by being Pritchett's "rapid reporter." By including yourself in the work in some way at the same time you're vanishing. By neither manhandling nor tidying up experience. By making a world that seems to have been found. The painter or writer has to signal that somewhere inside the work a controlling consciousness exists, but that in creating the world in miniature, the creator is quite aware of the artifice, and perhaps the sacrifice, involved. That he or she is cognizant of the larger world.

I like Mr. Pritchett's notion of the "rapid reporter or traveler with an eye for incident." Lincoln travels often, and when he does he keeps a sort of visual diary. Many of the things he records could be considered "incidents," I suppose, if you call a bird landing on a column an incident, or—this would certainly qualify—someone victimizing a woman. More often, though, the column, alone, is recorded because of its potential use in what will be, ultimately, a fictionalized "incident," or the painter's selective eye sketches a few figures that turn on a vase, while omitting others. Envy, envy: these might be sepia ink sketches. And the ordinary looks so fresh, so surprising when simplified. Omissions change everything.

Sometimes Lincoln makes a visual note on a cocktail napkin. I can't tell you the guilt I've suffered, pulling out the wash and looking at the remains of a pen-stained, shredded napkin. We're very different: I try not to observe and not to hear, trusting (perhaps wrongly; how would I know?) that the important things stored away in the subconscious will emerge again when and if needed. I depend on that, as a working method: when I least expect it, my fortune (YOU HAVE MILES TO GO) will float up to the surface of the Magic 8 Ball, so to speak. But most things get lost, no matter how indelibly drawn, whether put down with pen and ink on a drawing pad or carefully placed in all but the final draft. My revised pages are filled with extraneous, crossed-out sentences; Lincoln fills pocket-sized drawing pads with visual or verbal notes to himself that are seldom heeded or consulted, but so what? In registering them, or recording them, they lodged in our brains and might be useful when least expected. (Lincoln is a great mimic, by the way: his talent is to have observed some tiny quirk others would overlook, and to use that to define his subject.)

We both seem to filter, to mix and match, to recall in tranquility, but mostly—let's be honest—to dutifully imagine that we will eventually write or depict something, and then we forget it. Lincoln isn't a reporter: even if what he paints is familiar, he has to defamiliarize it so things can be seen as new. I think his shifting away from one perspective—adding information, subtracting, refusing to mark each transition, fine-tuning—is first and foremost not playing to himself, not provoking just to provoke, or reassuring just to create something beautiful, to placate. He's doing what he does not in order to get an answer ("What do you talk about?") but to pose a question, which, by implication, makes the audience better able to articulate their own uncertainty. In so doing, they enter the world of the paintings.

In his paintings you might be drawn to the Charlottesville you've always known. Or the place might be one element, while the text and subtext offer something unexpected. In many of them, you'll probably see a place simultaneously familiar and unfamiliar—because that's the way the painter views the world: there's a necessity for the familiar to be reenergized by being defamiliarized; he sometimes does an improvisation so astute it stabilizes the original. At times he might also use complexity to get at a simple truth, or present something obvious that becomes less so, when seen more clearly over time. In any case, along with being what it is, the work will also exist as a portrait of a person—a Gemini, by the way—who accepts Charlottesville's mutability as a partial definition of its familiarity, so that the unlikeliness of arrival becomes one of the painter's points of departure. Your self-questioning guide will have packed both a spyglass and a prism in the travel bag.

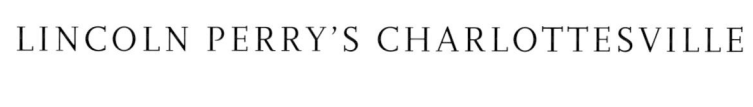

LINCOLN PERRY'S CHARLOTTESVILLE

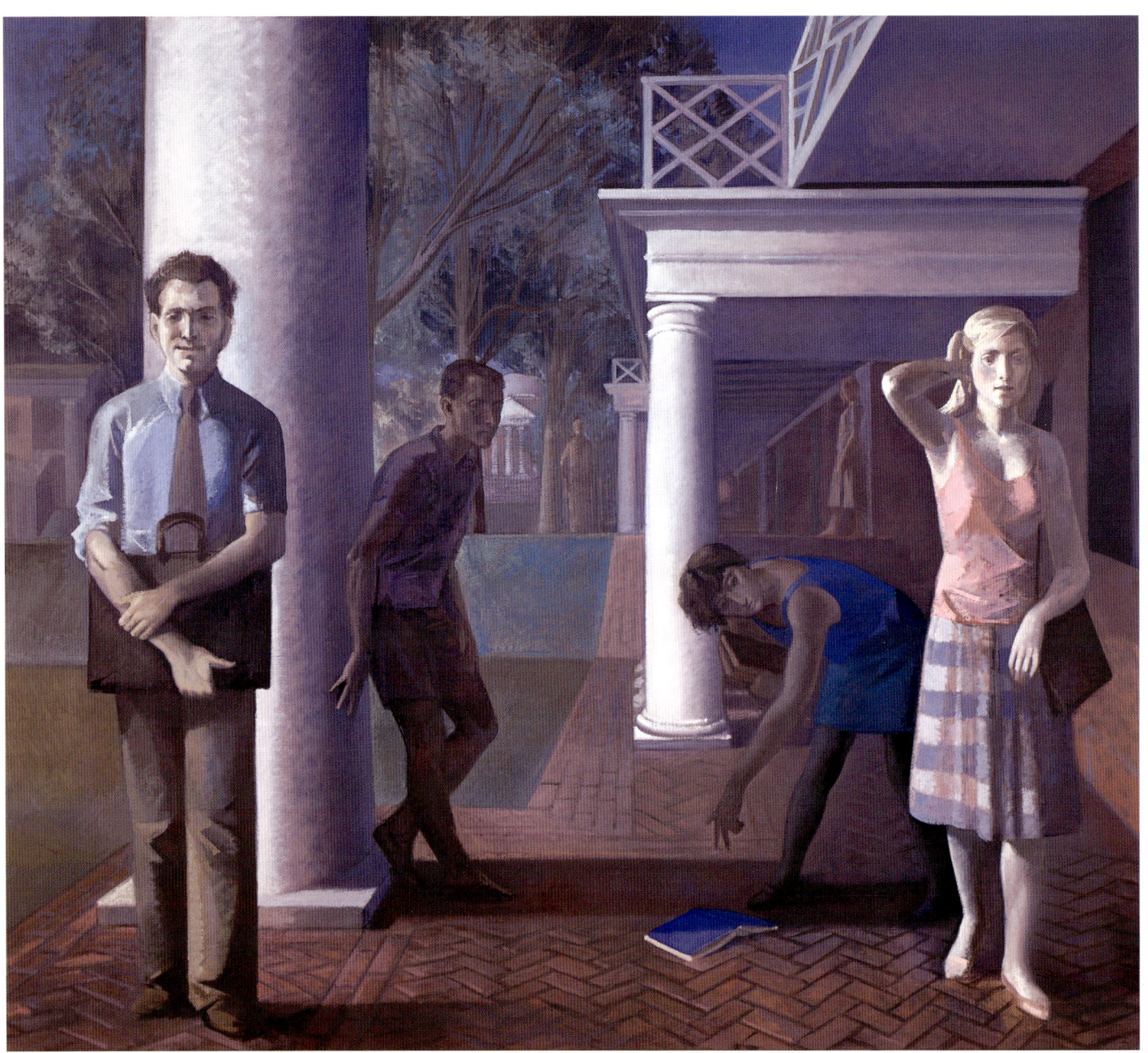

2

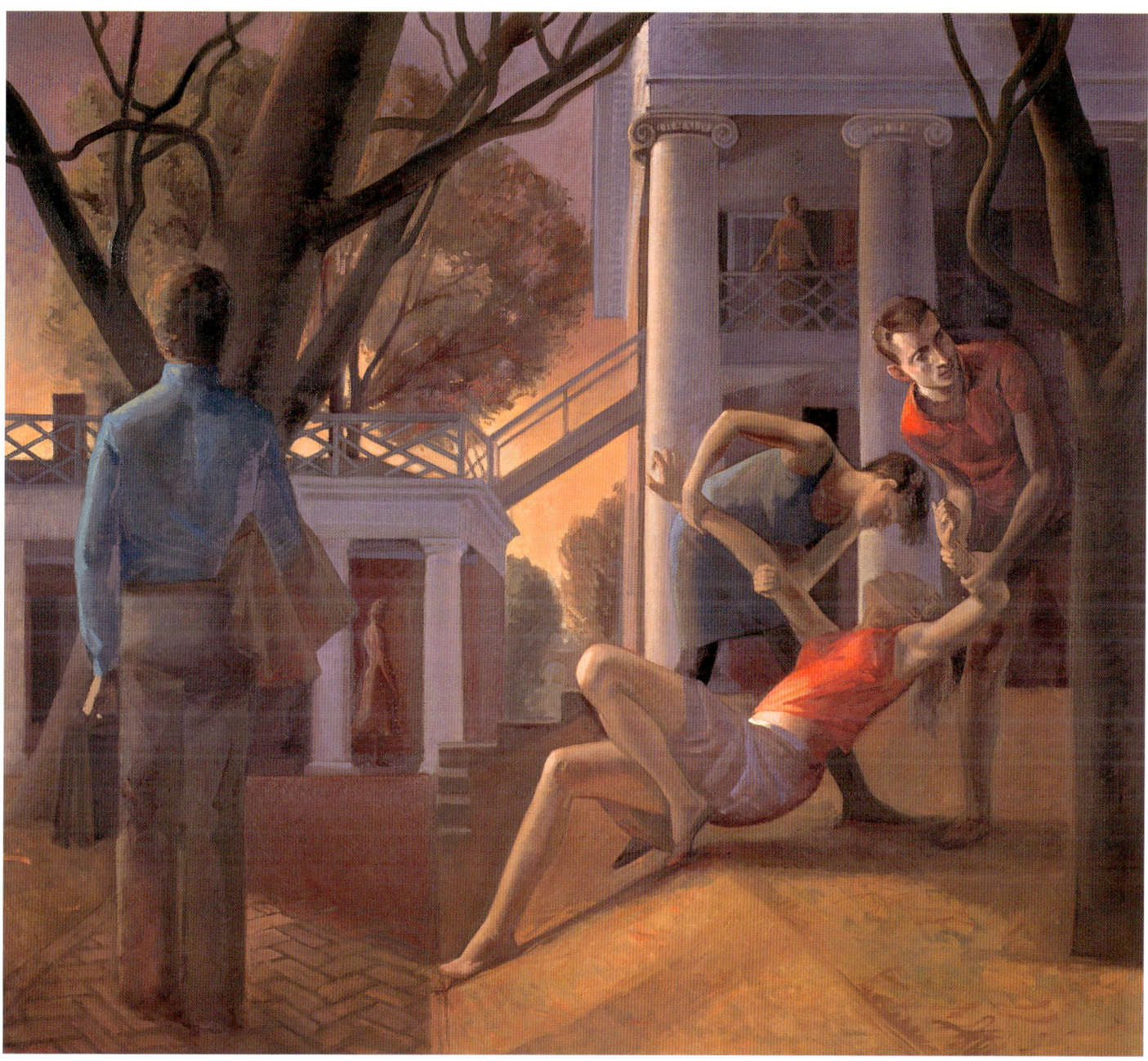

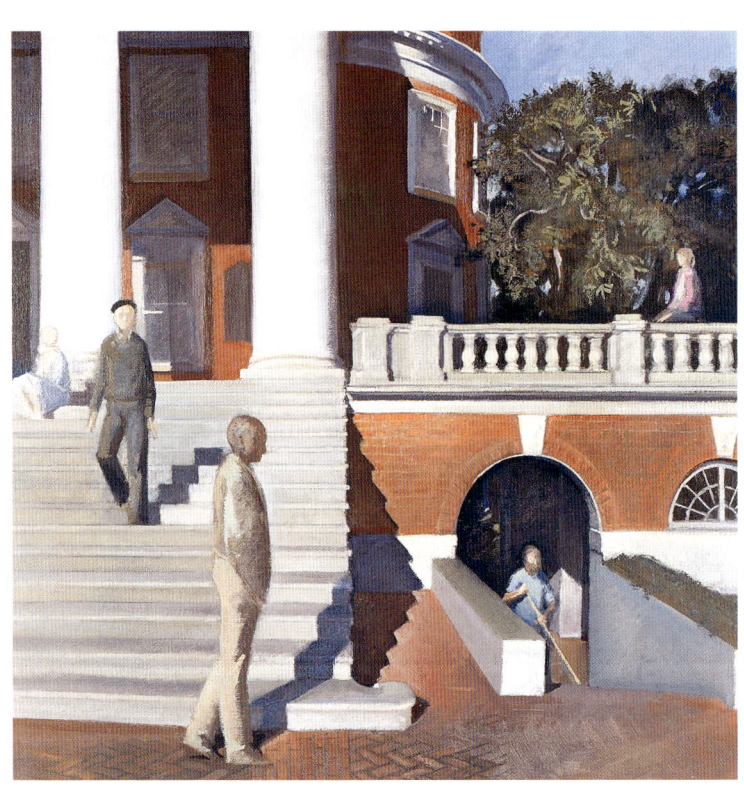

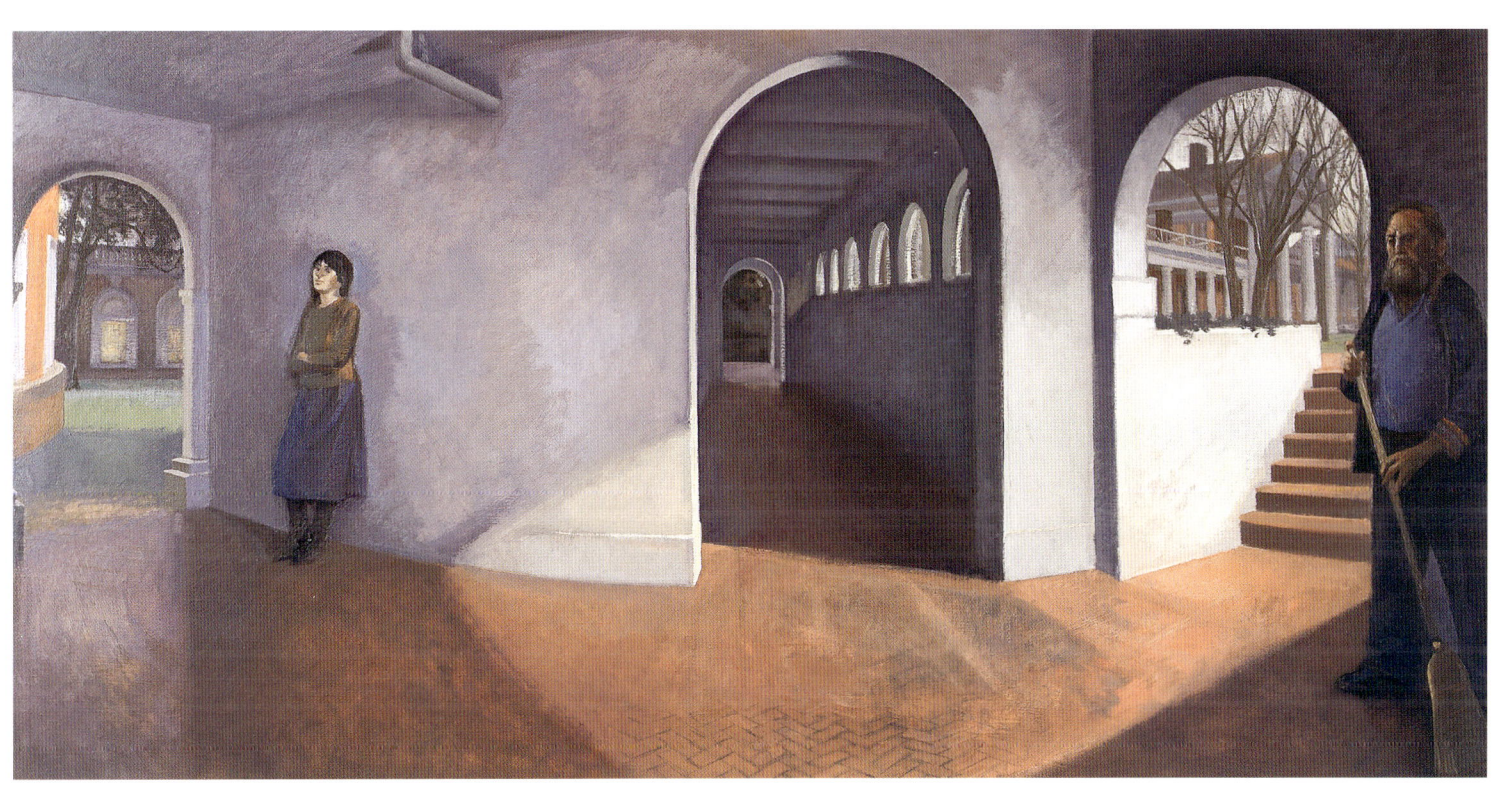

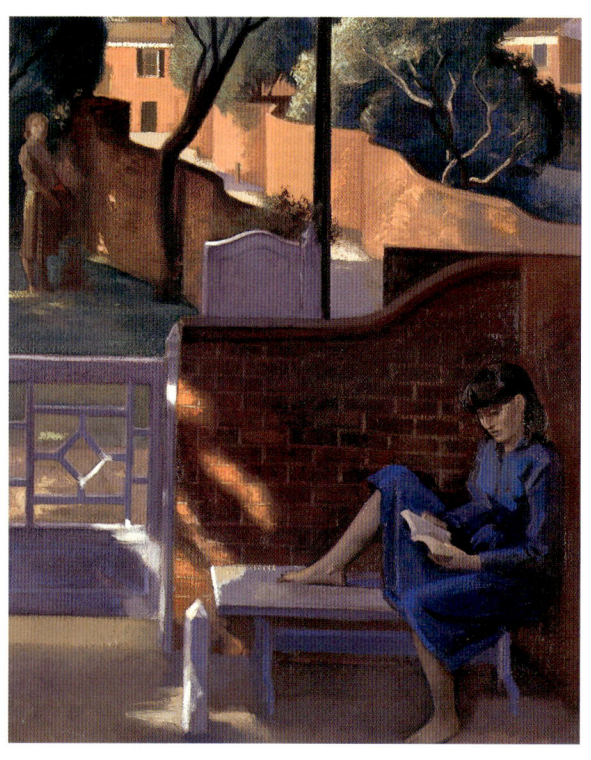
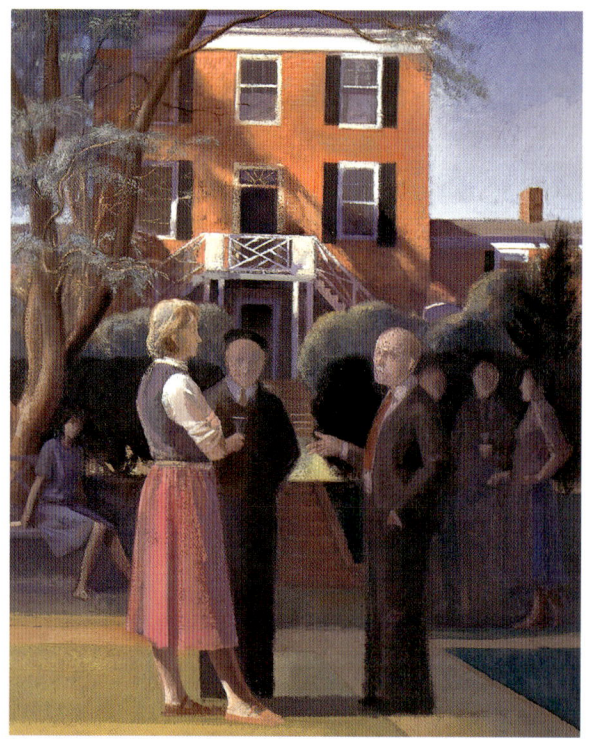

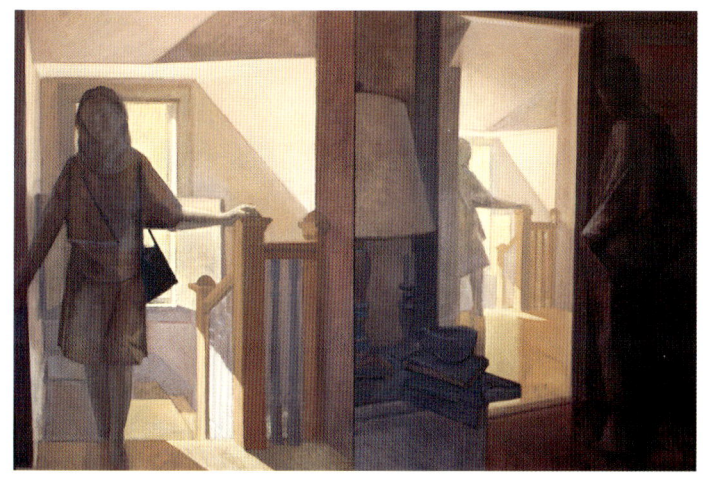
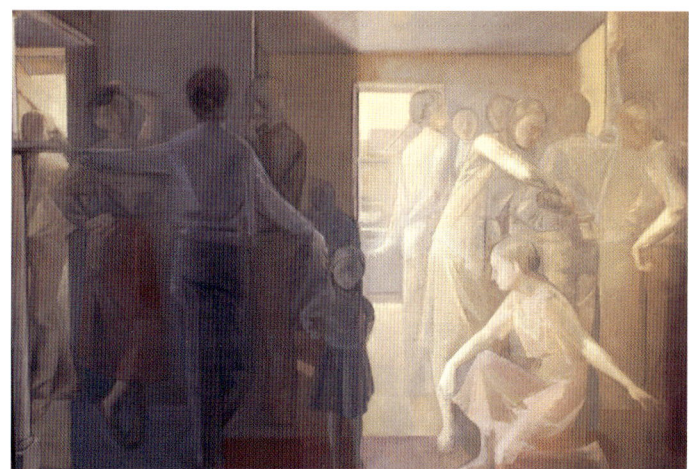
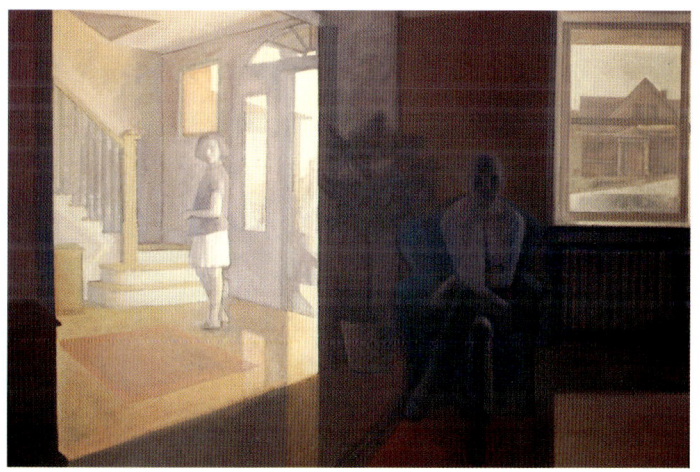
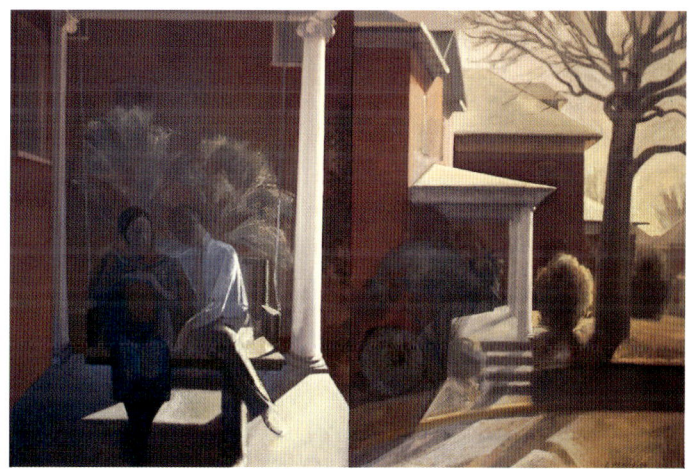

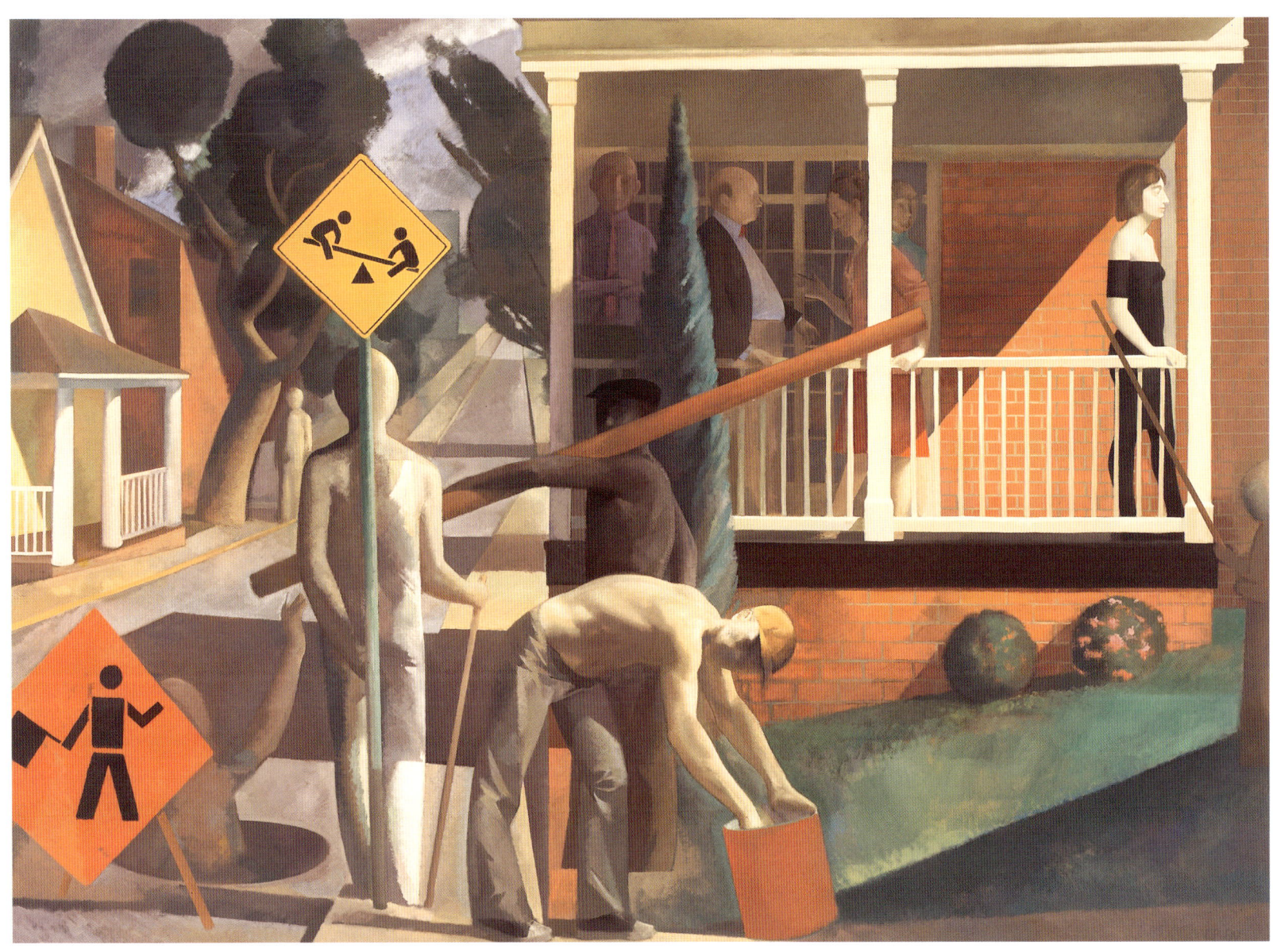

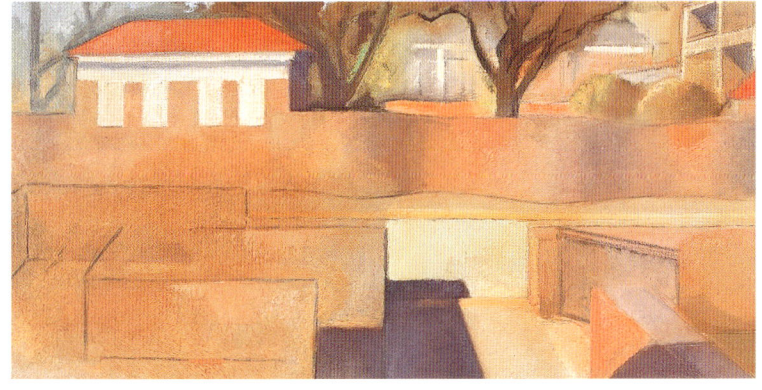
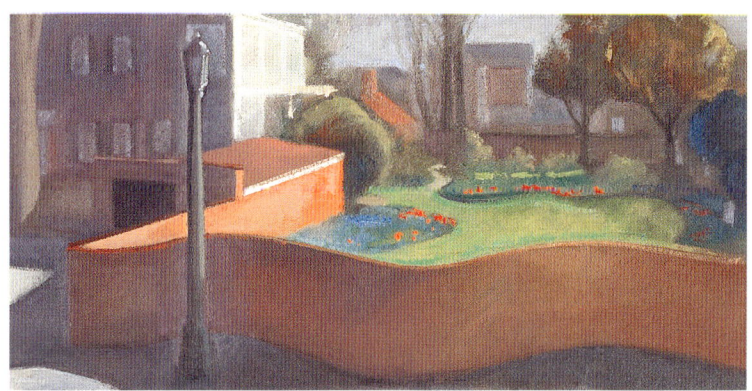
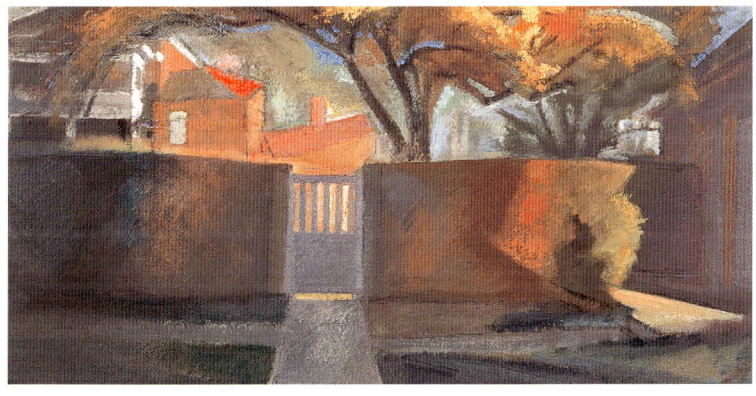
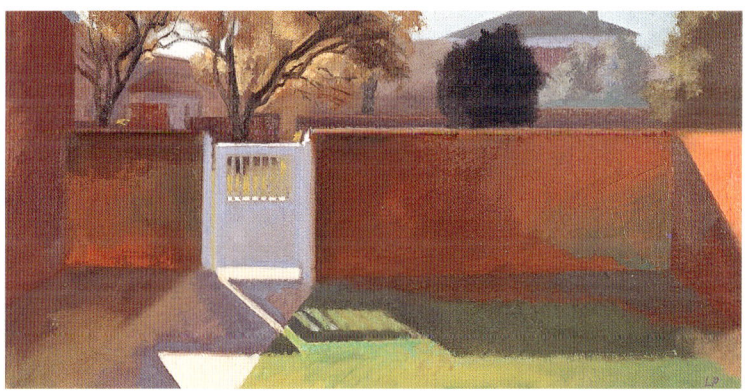

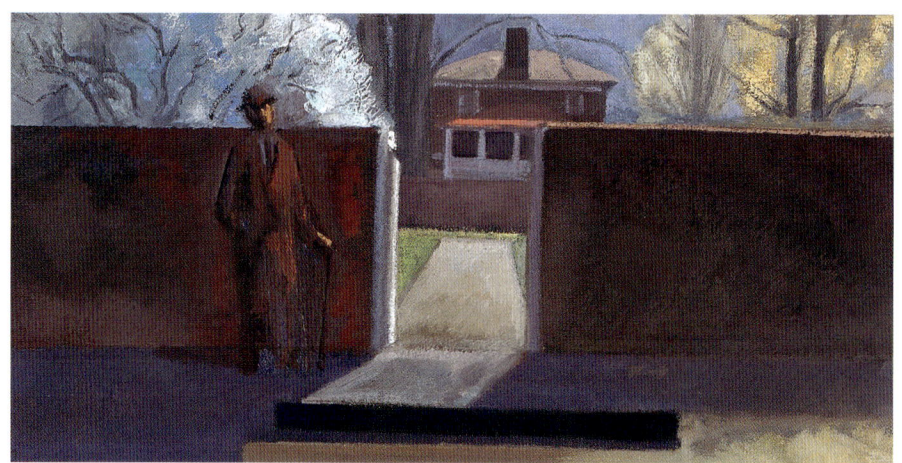

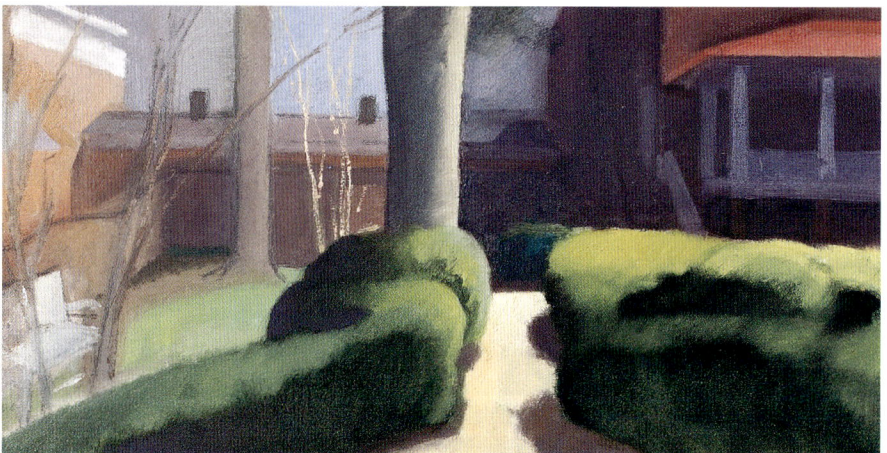

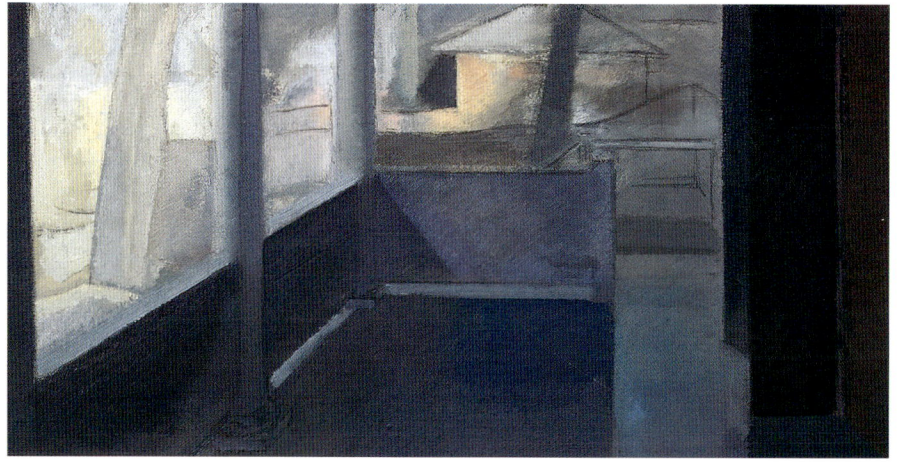

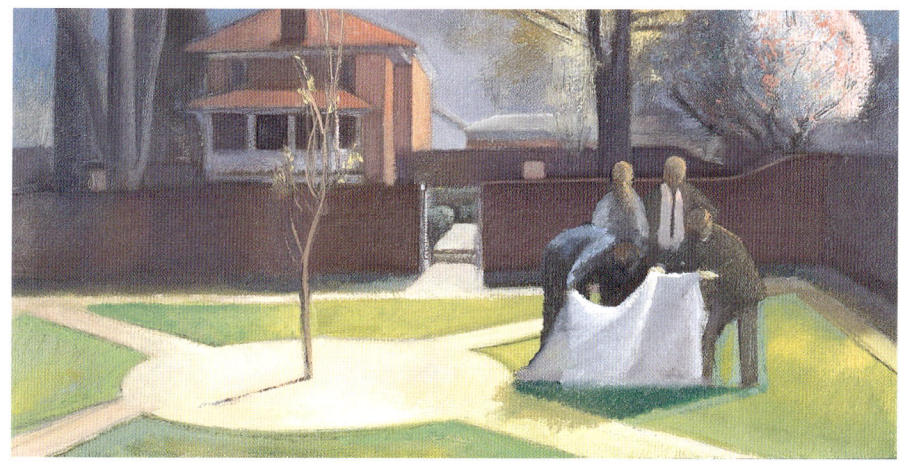

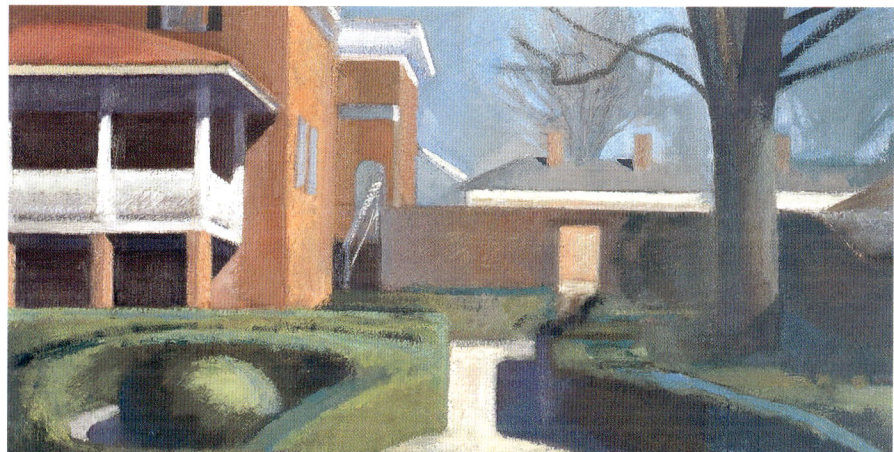

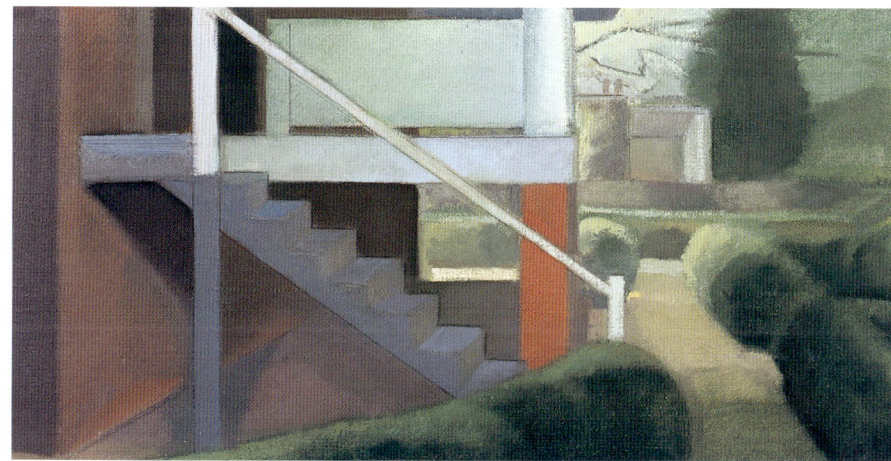

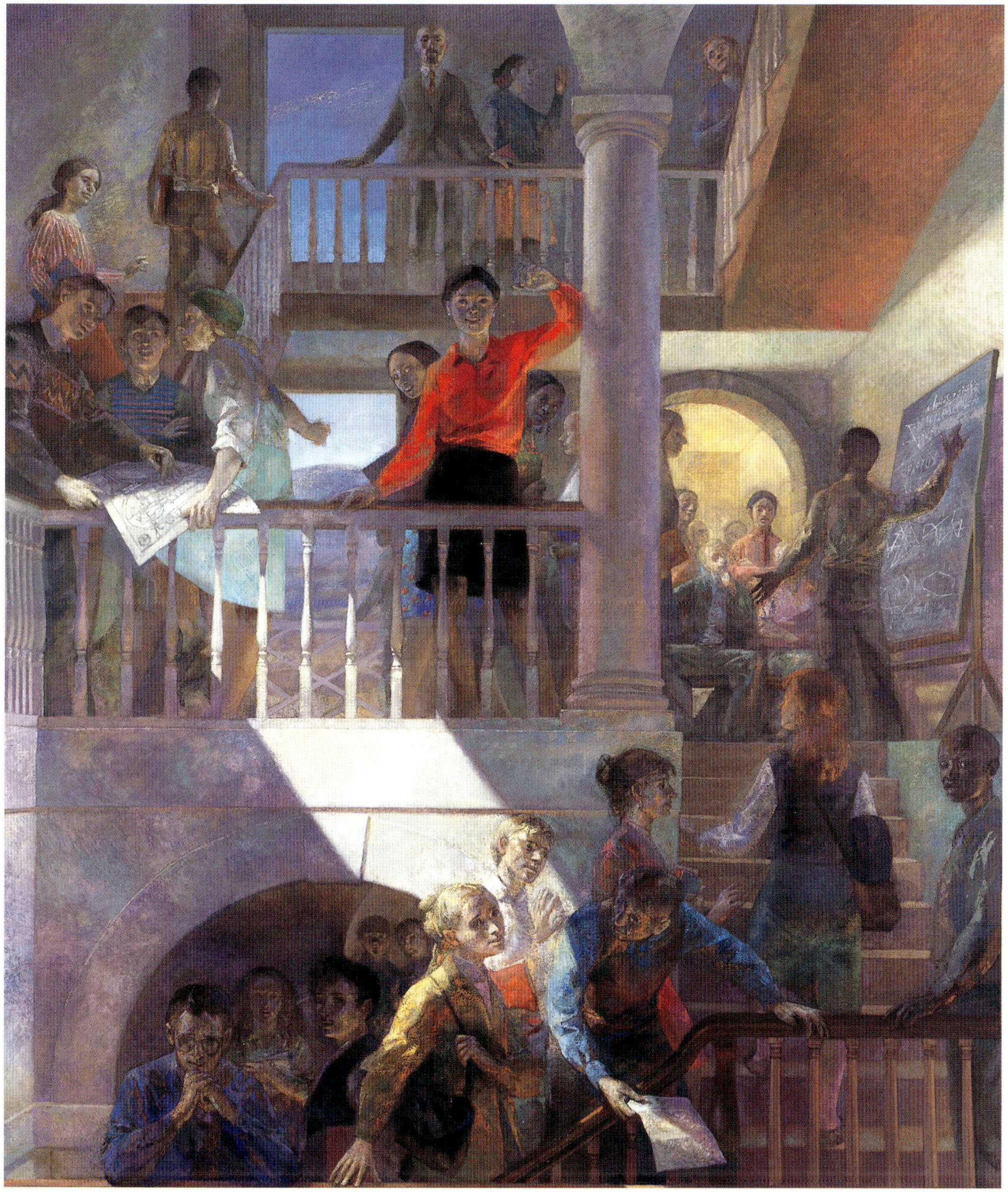

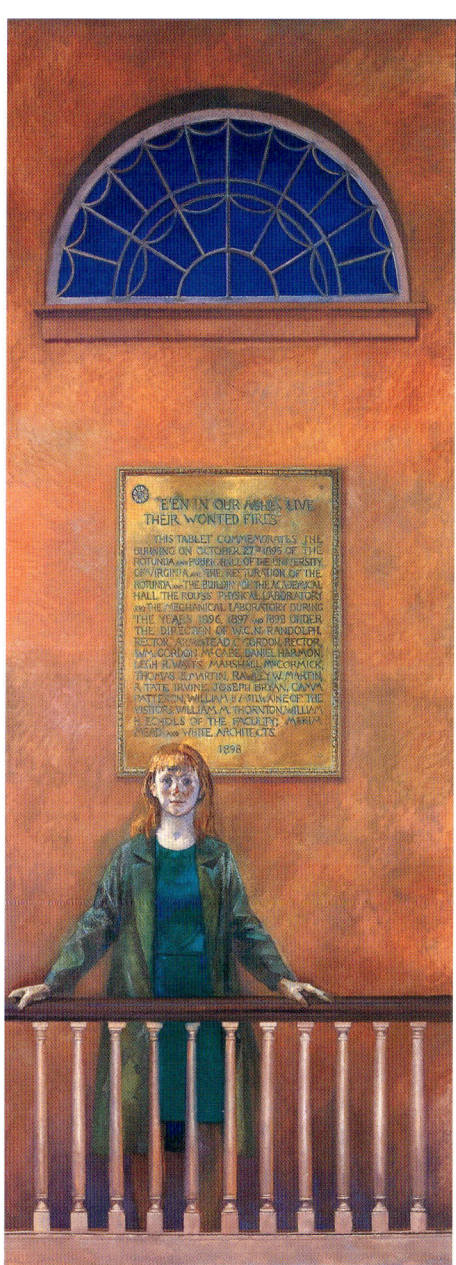

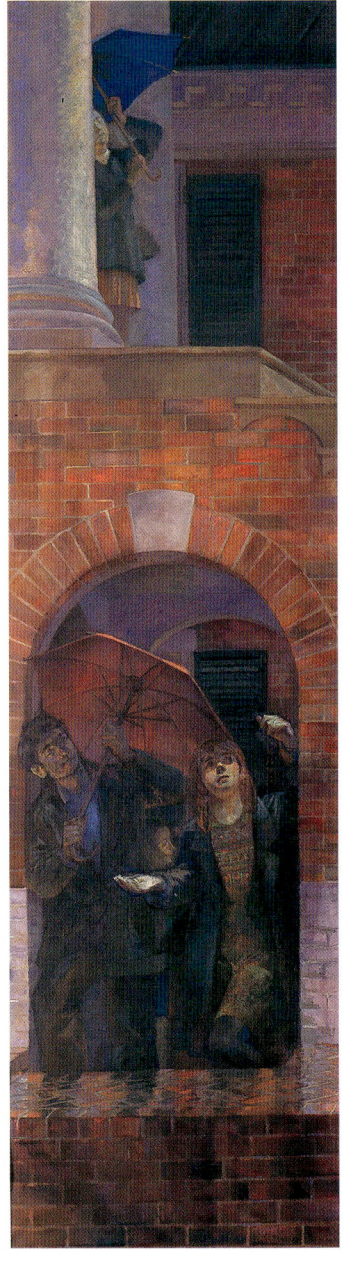
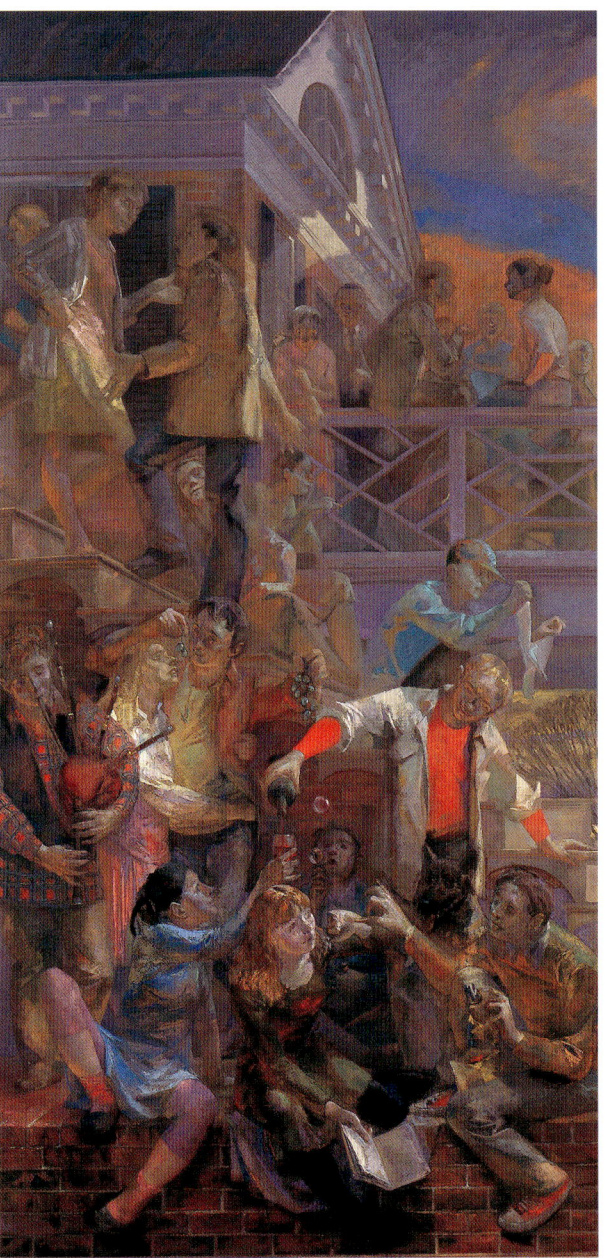
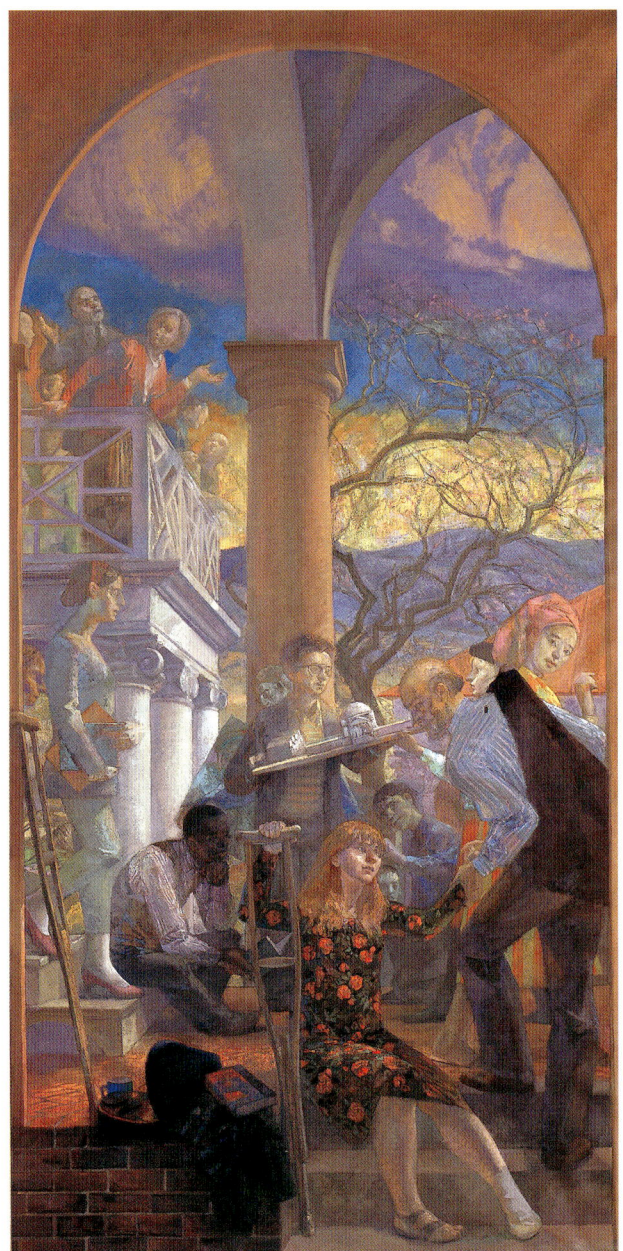

14

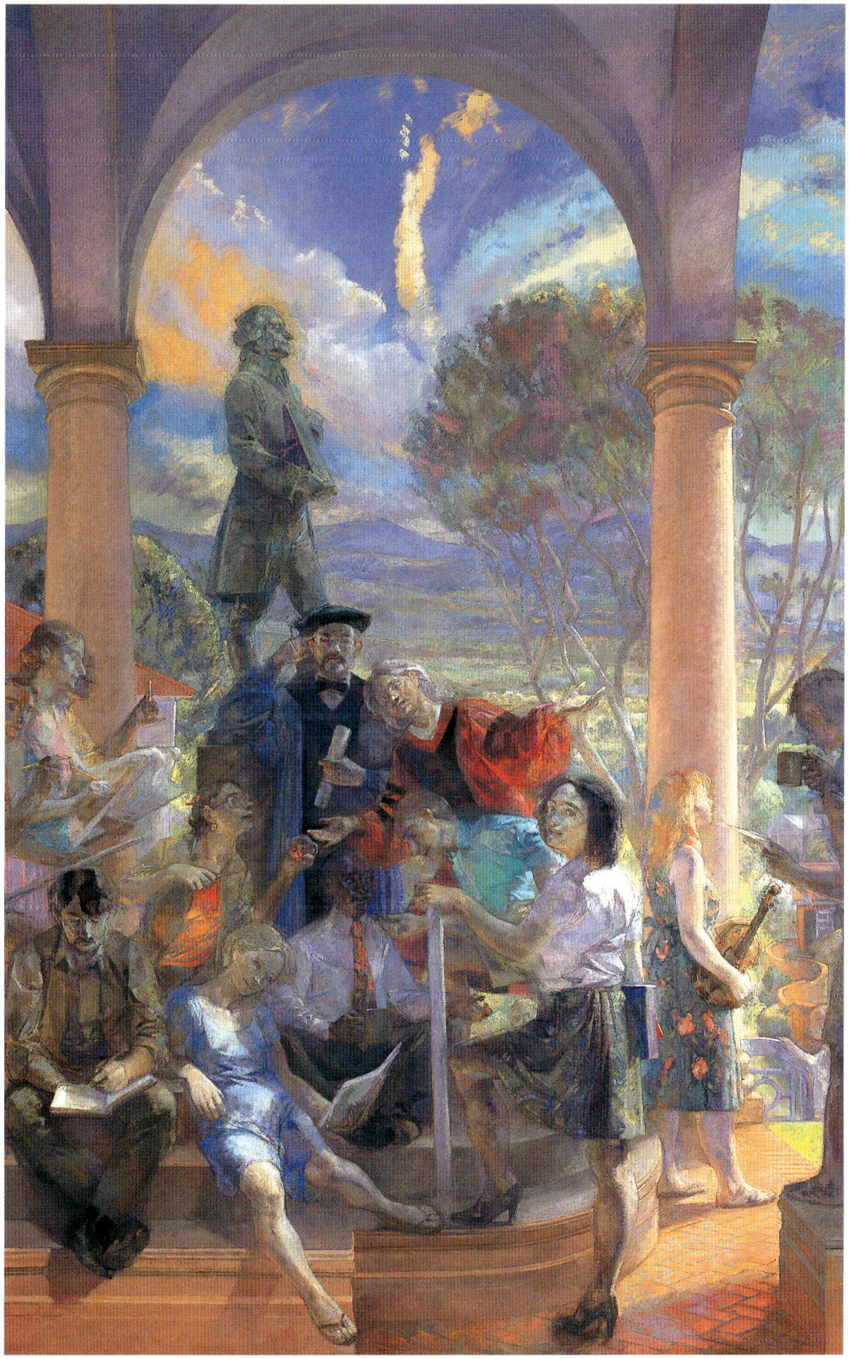

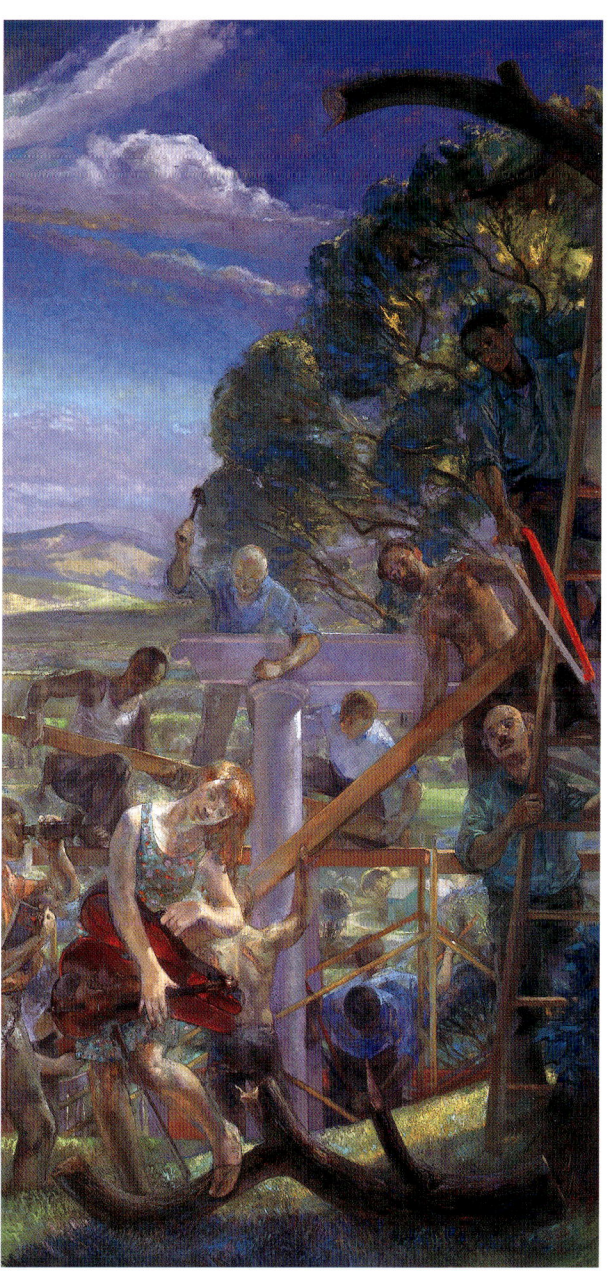

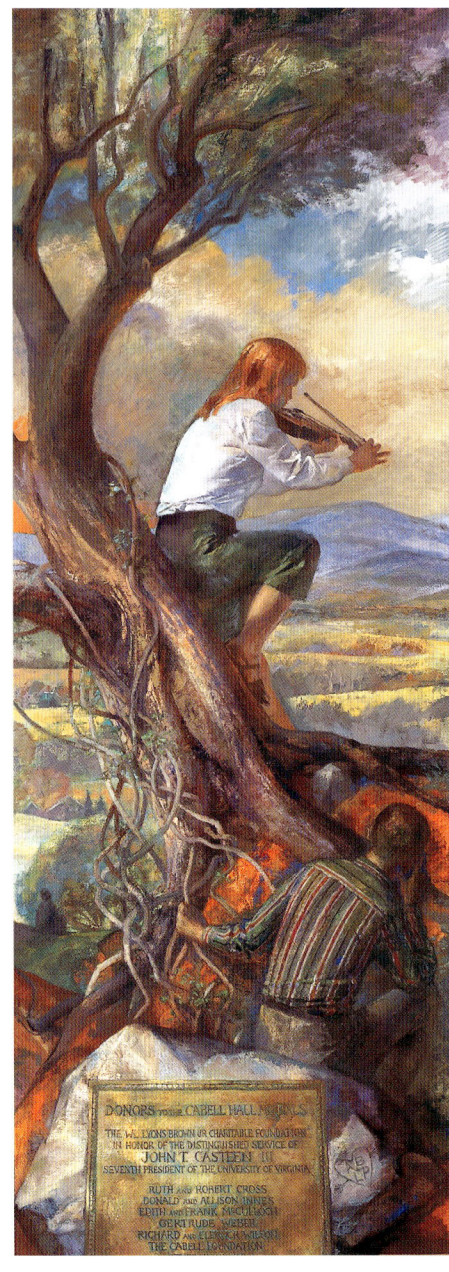

16

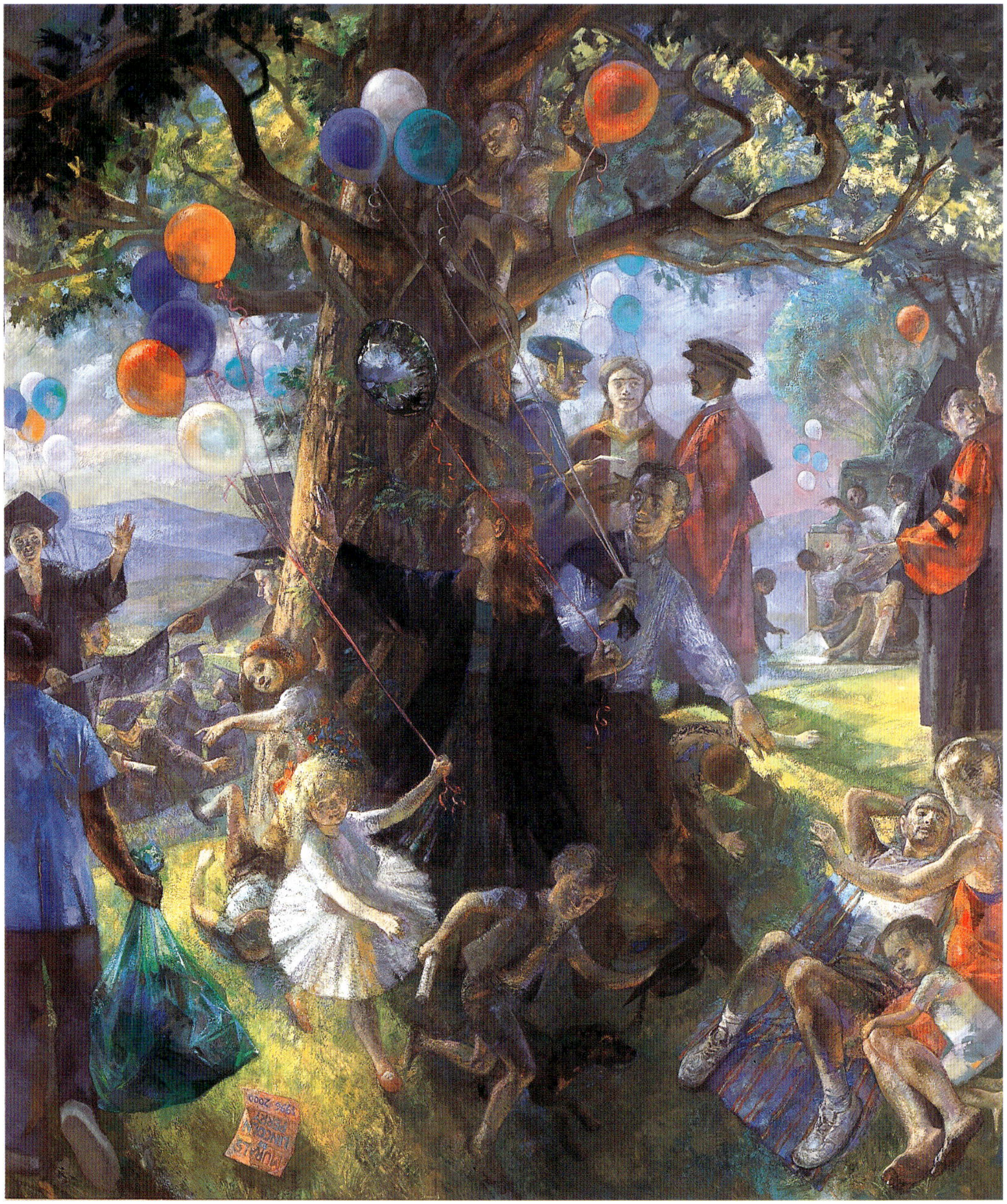

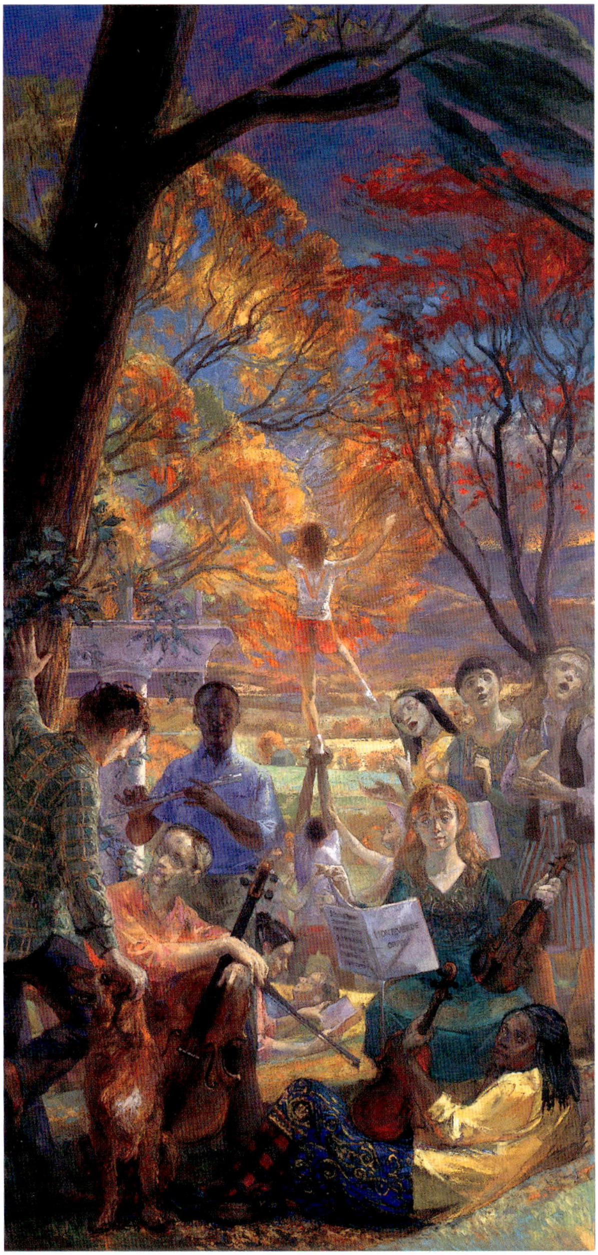

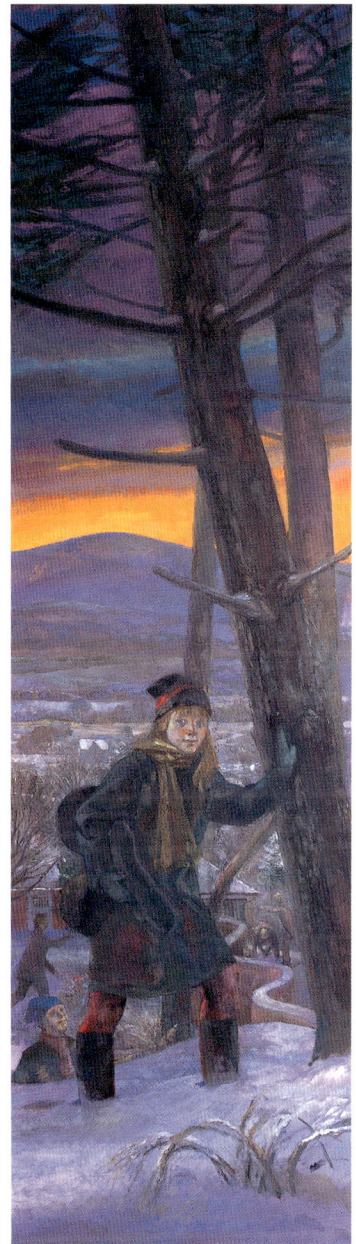

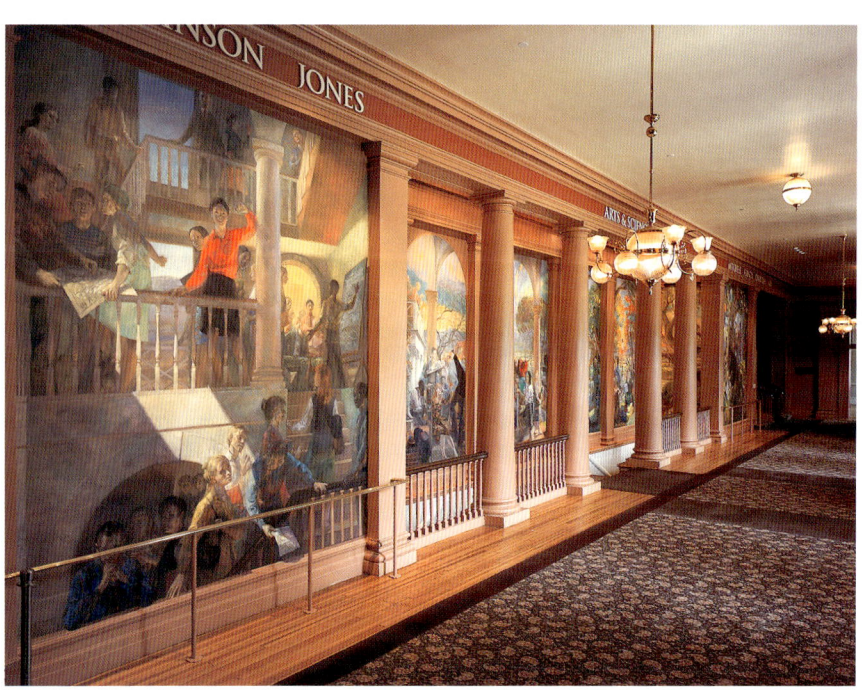

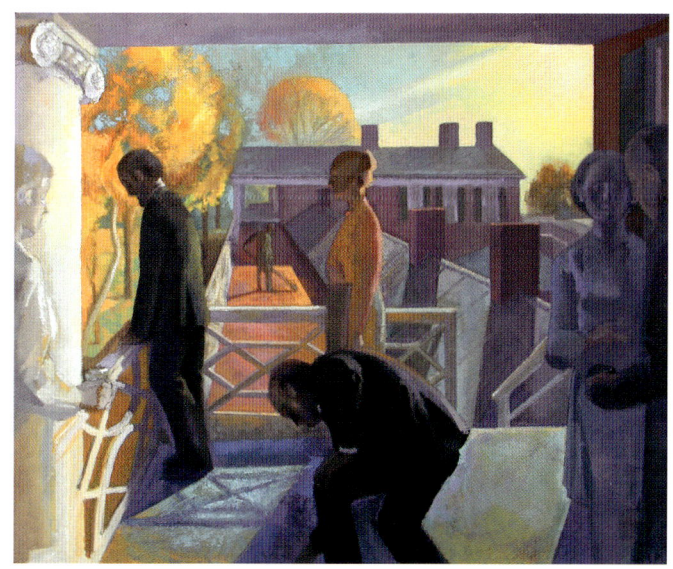
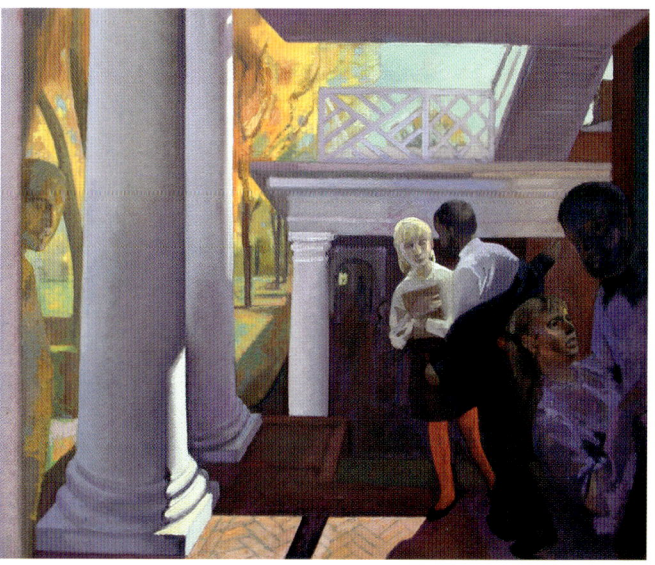
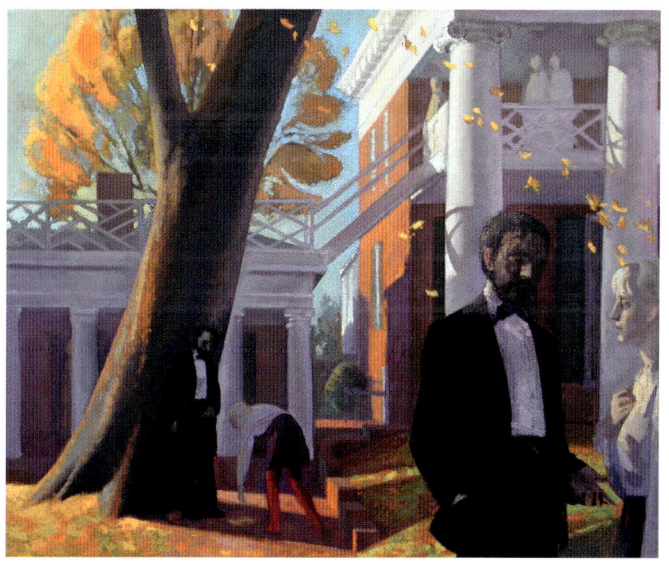
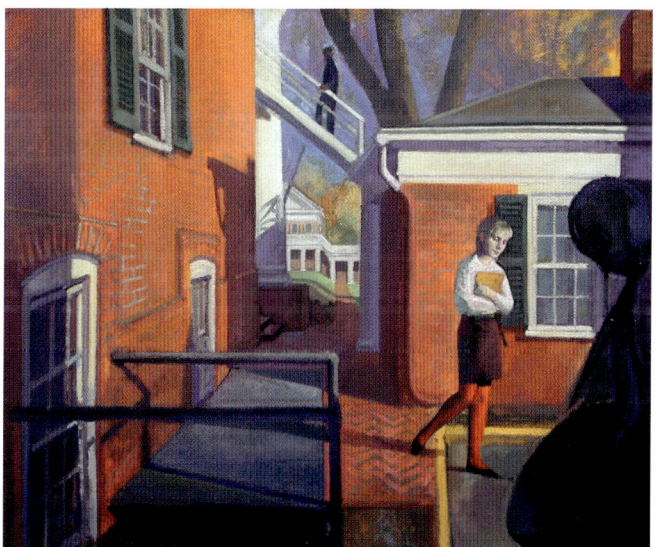

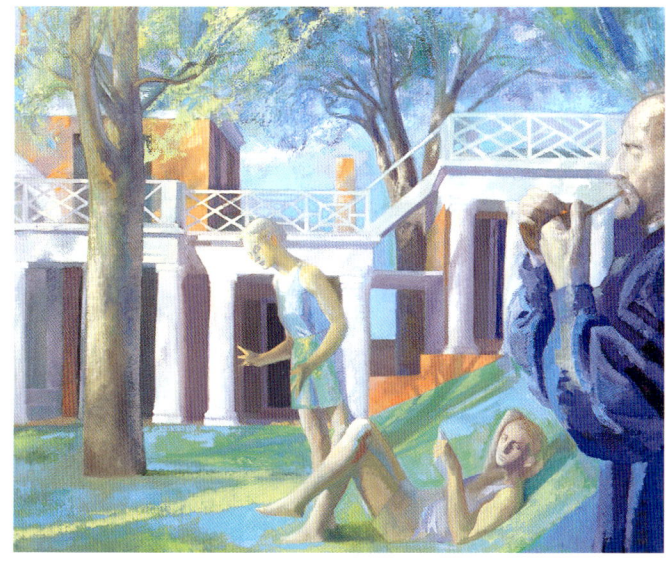
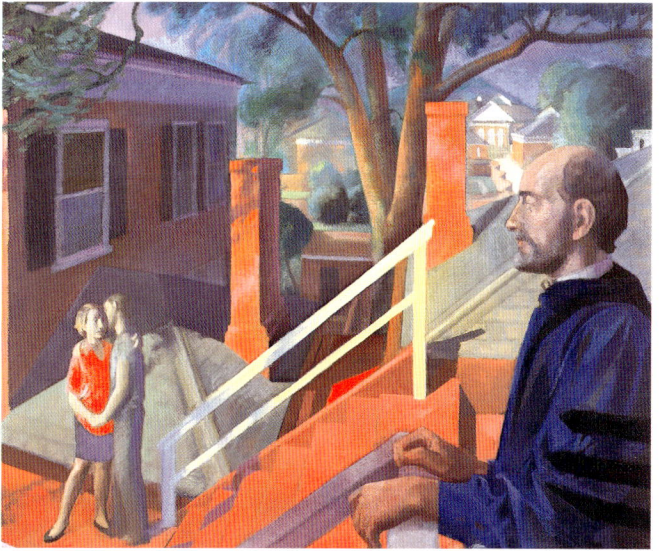
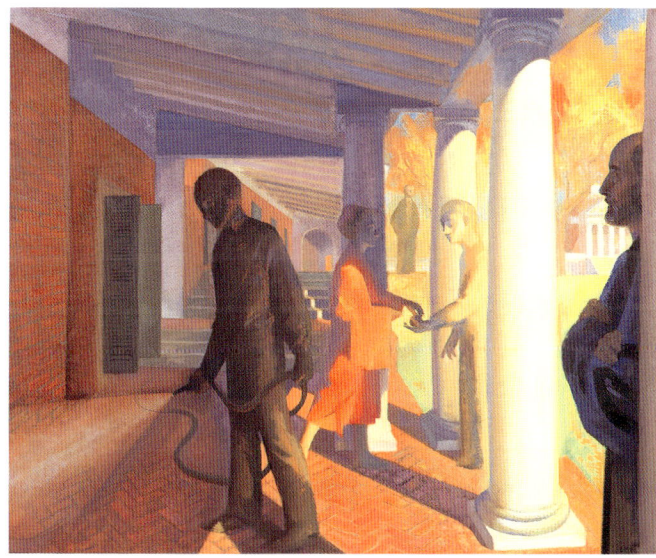
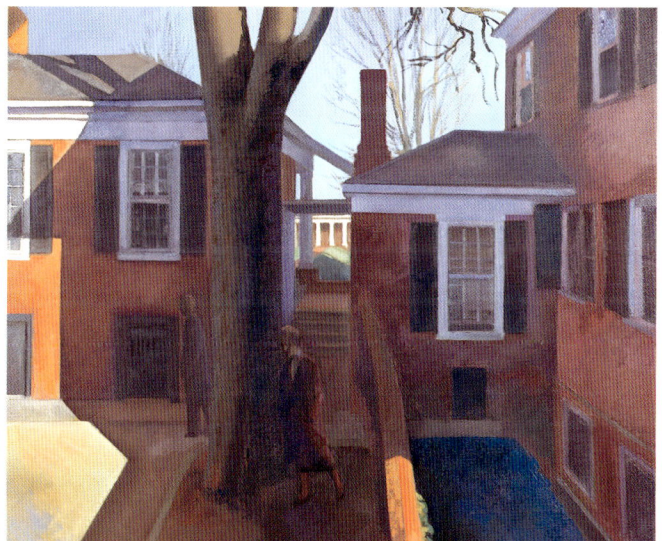

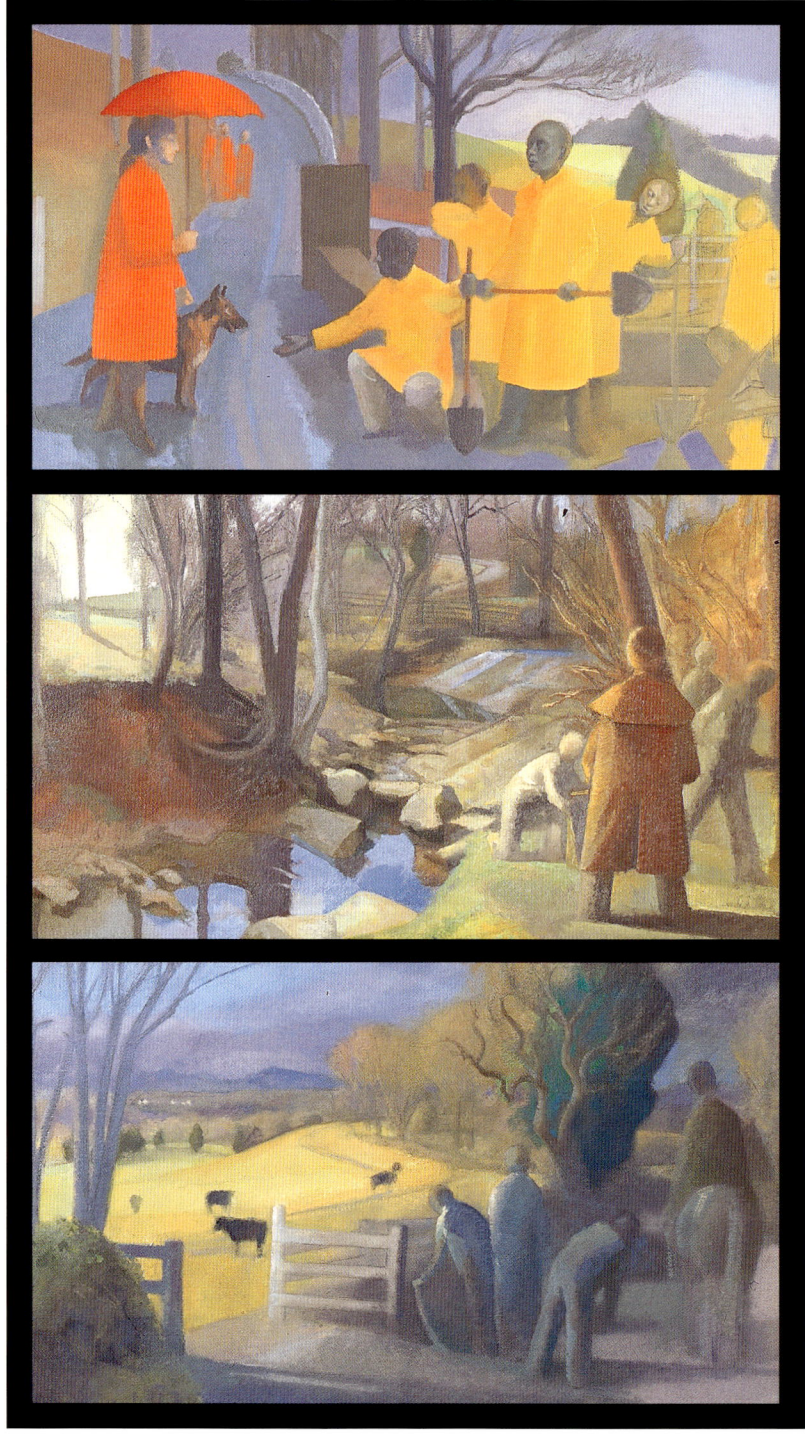

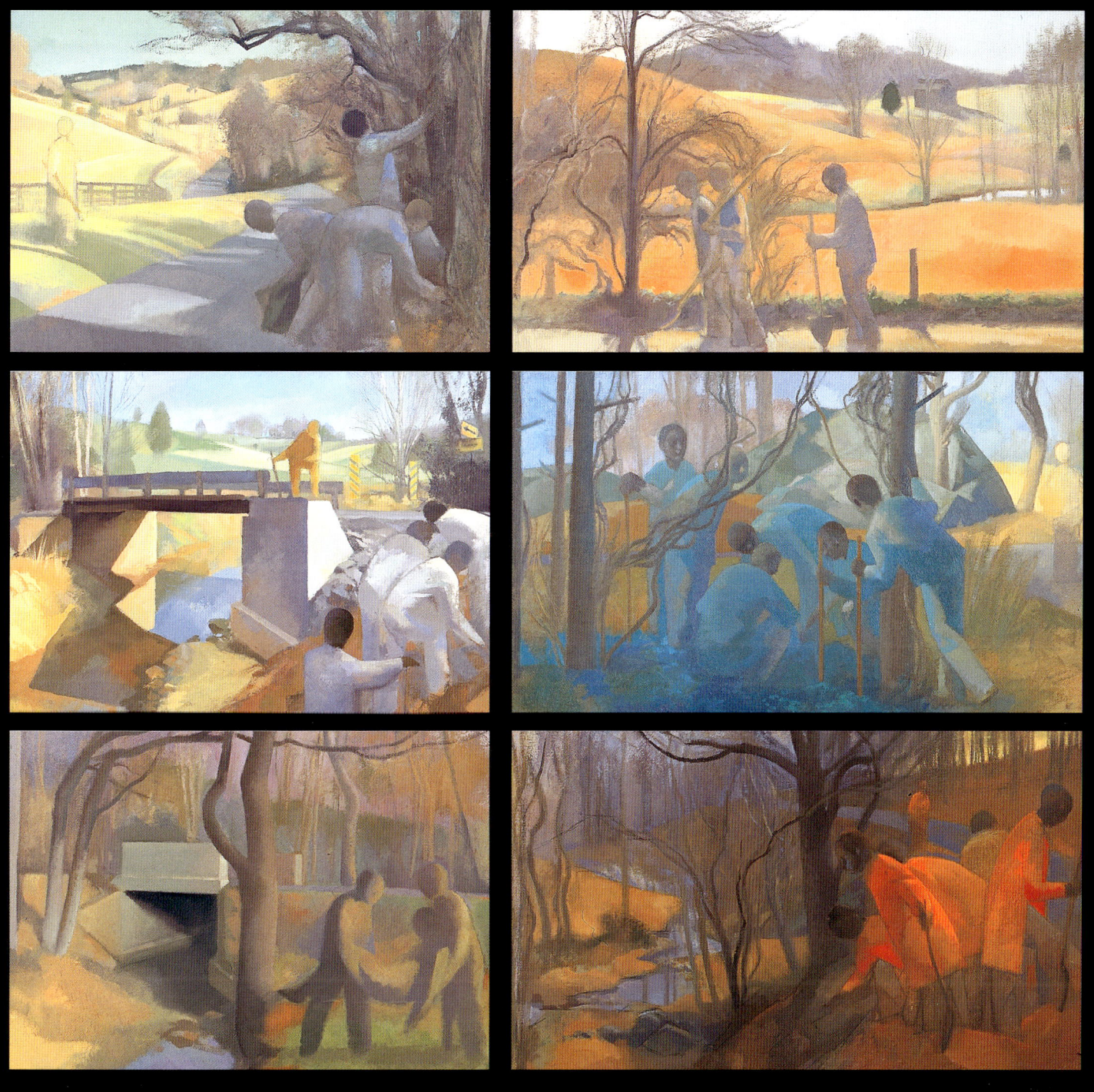

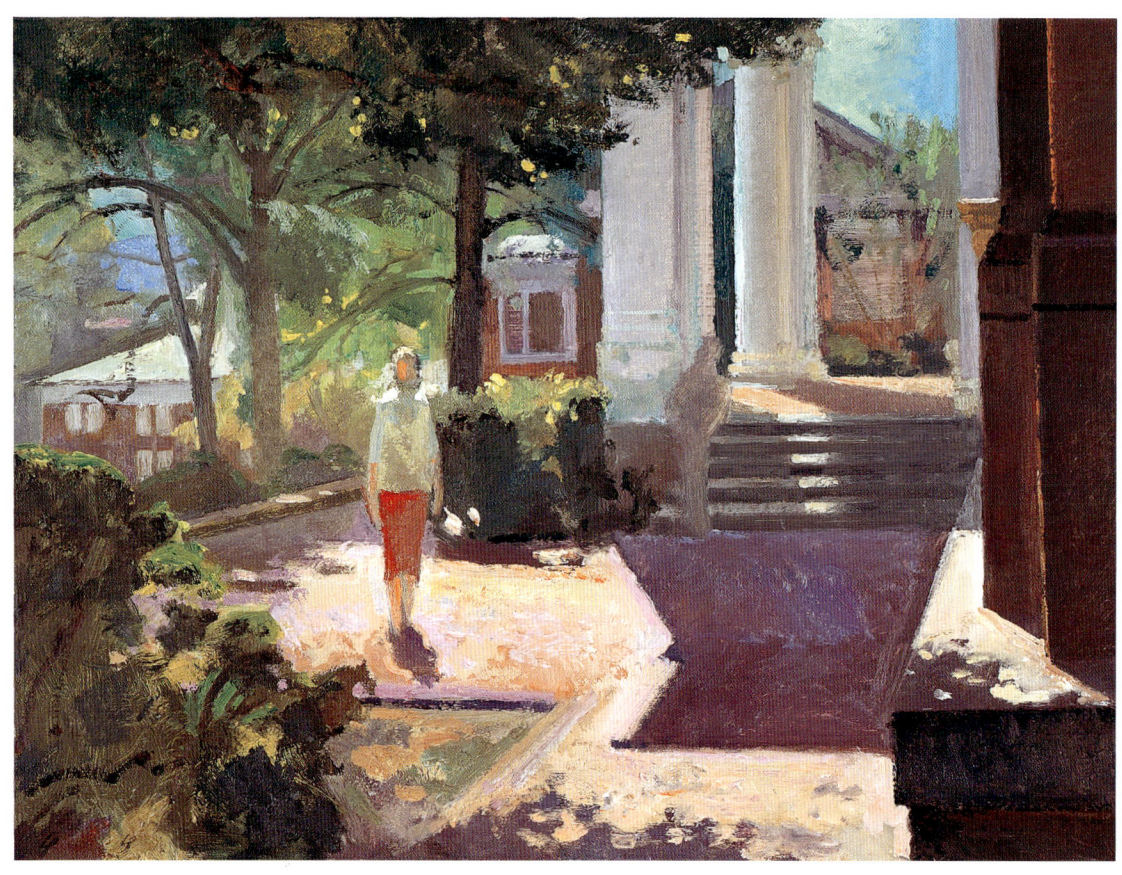

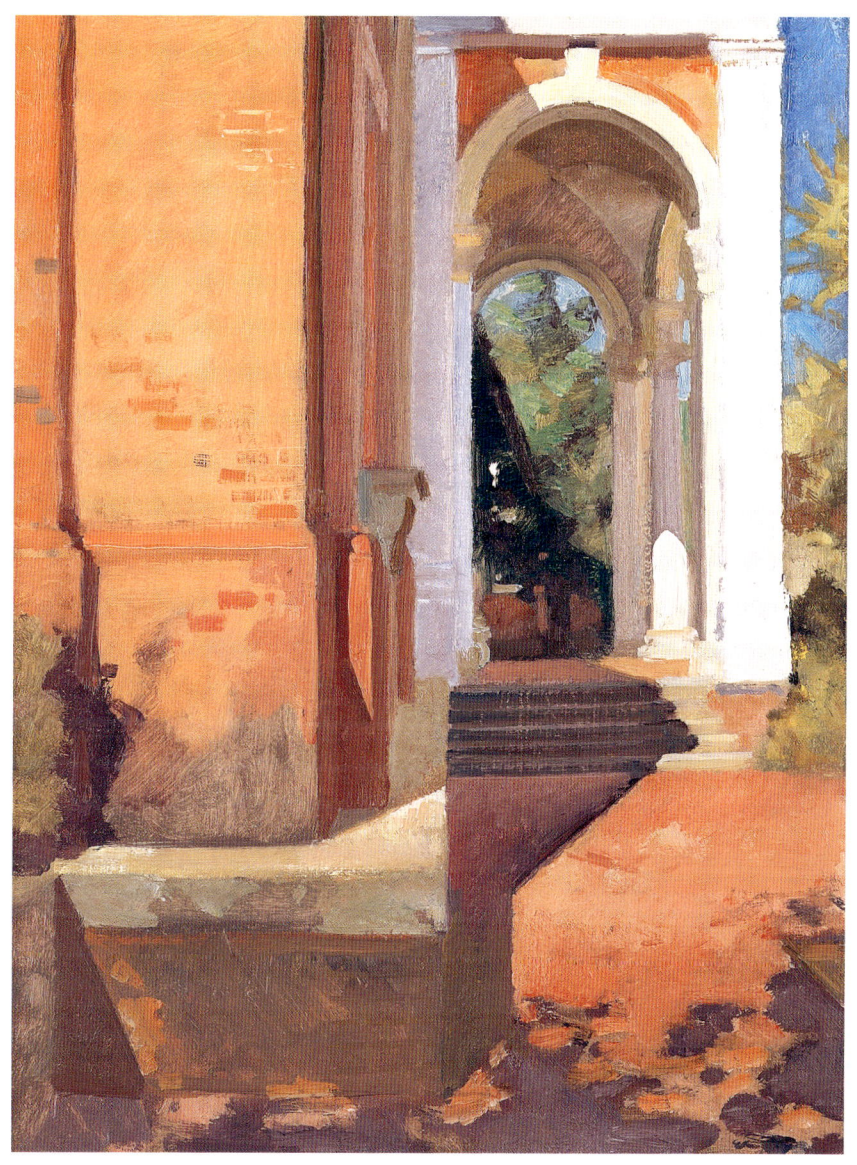

23

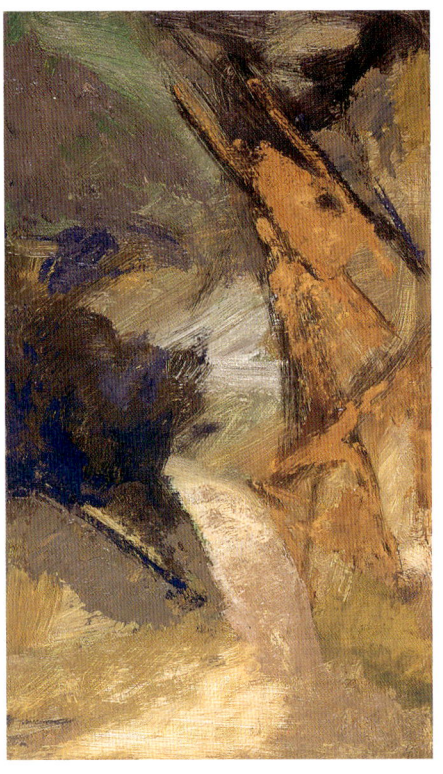 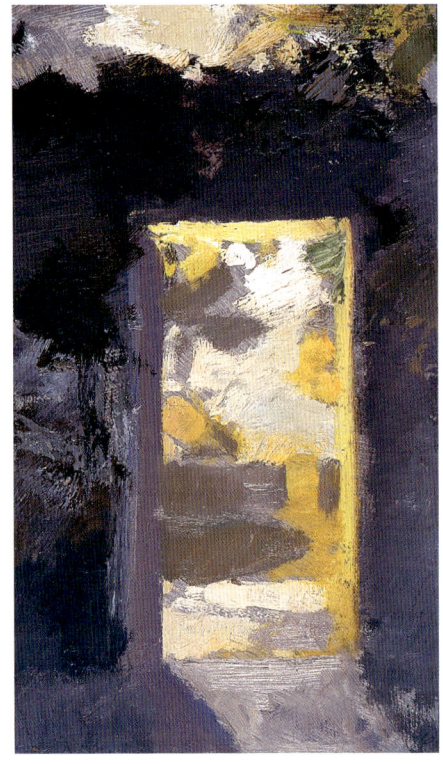 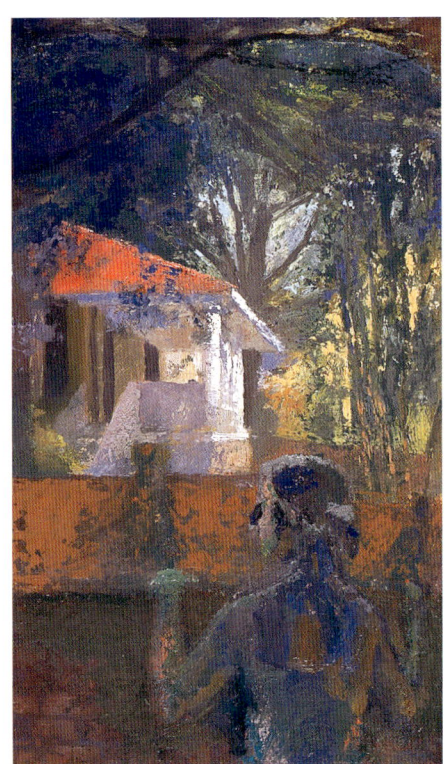

24

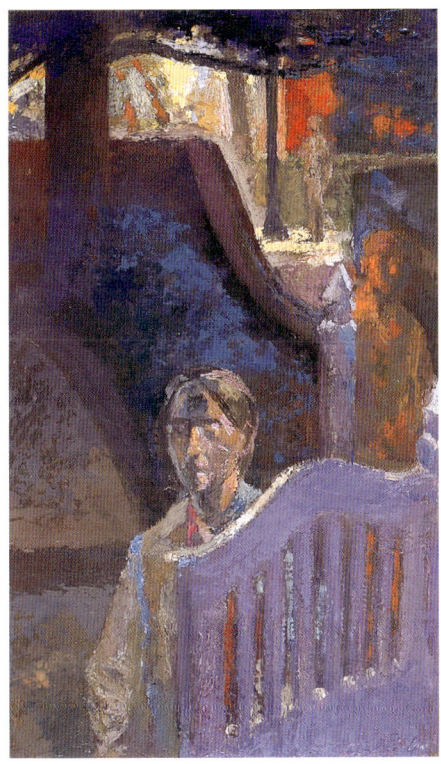
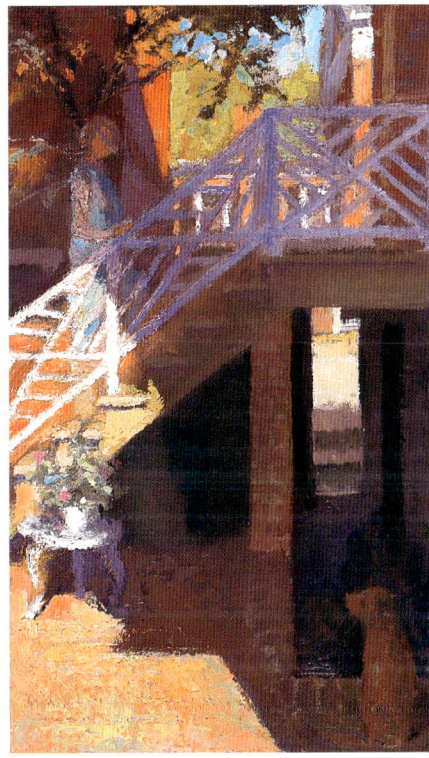
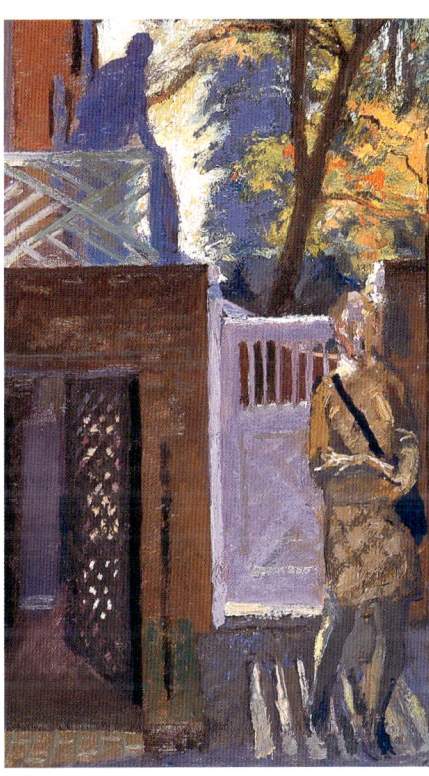

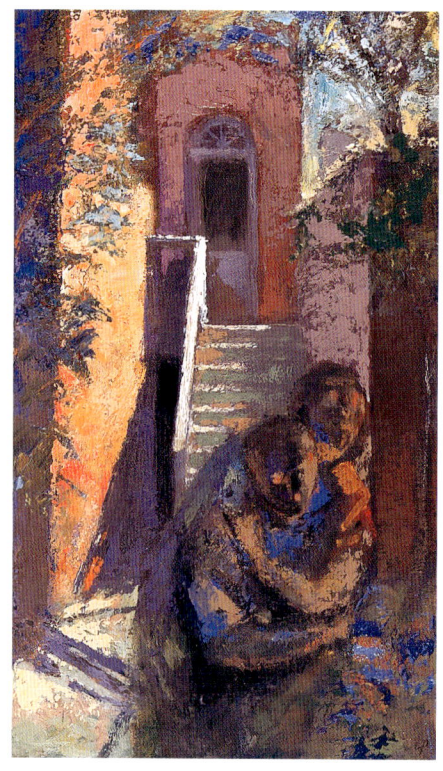
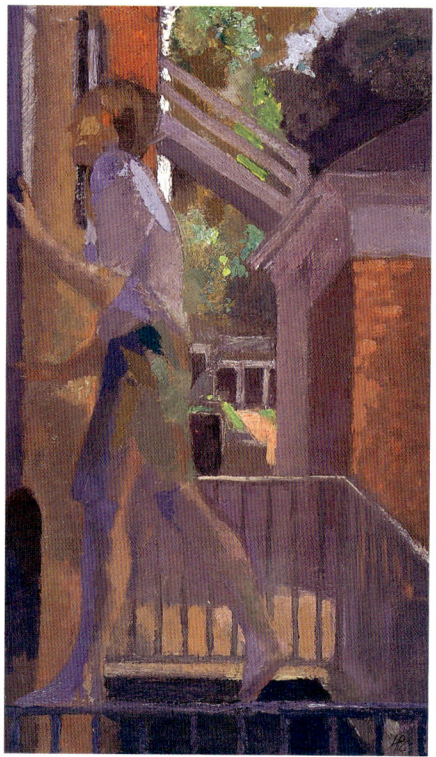
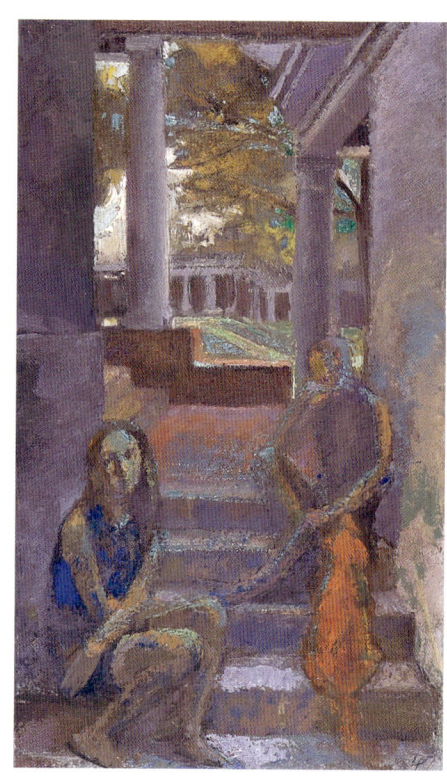

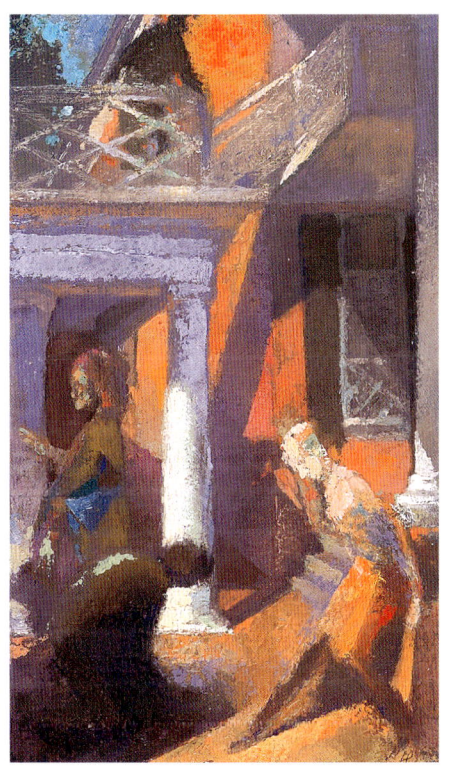 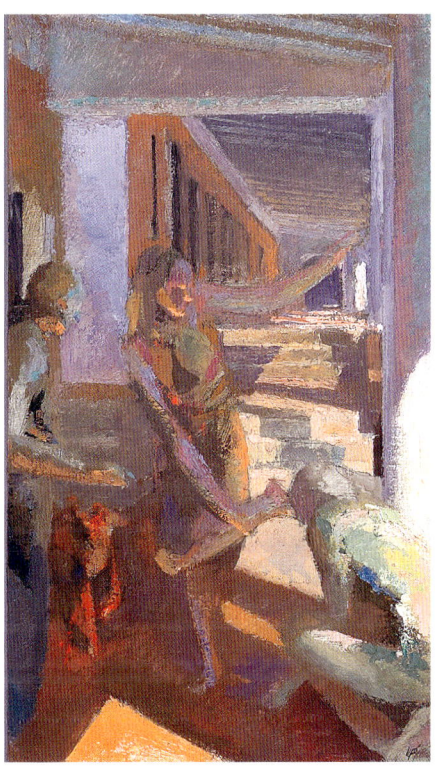 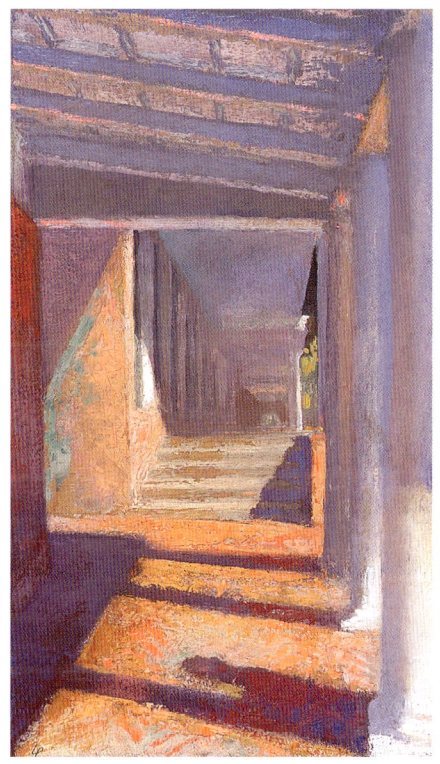

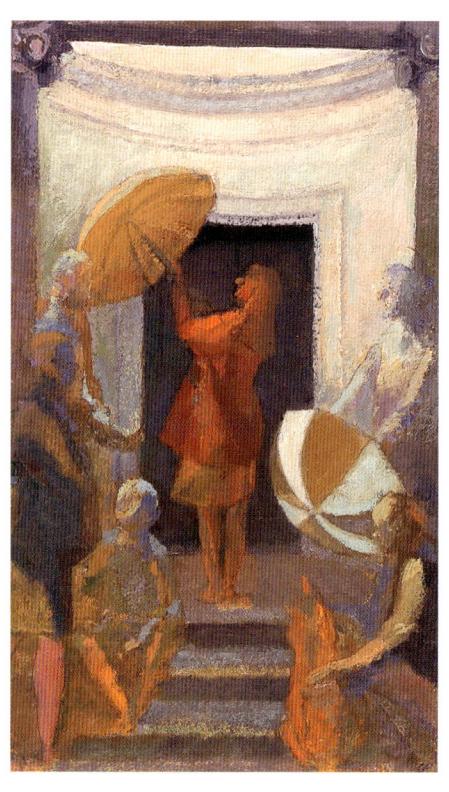 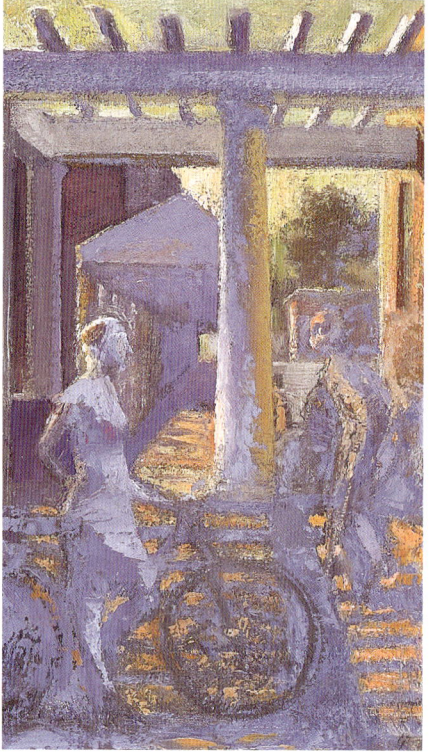 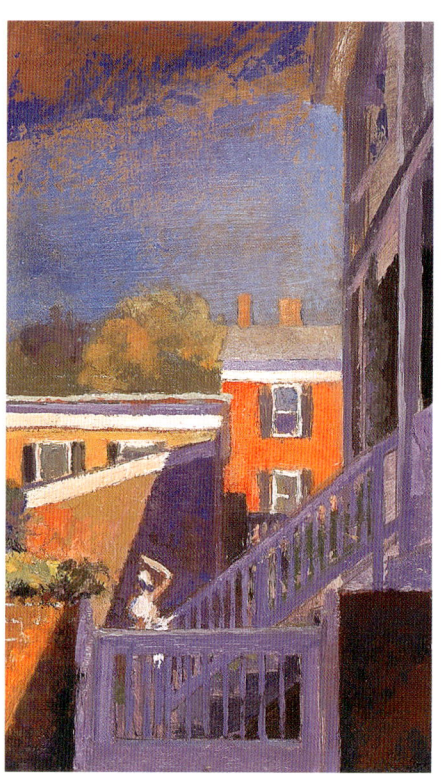

28

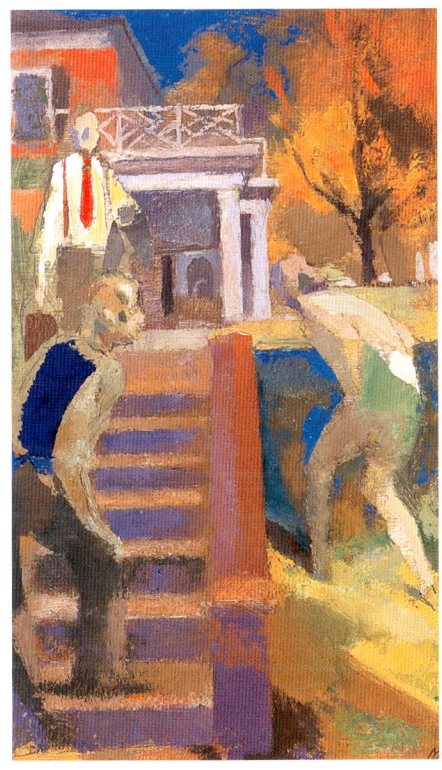
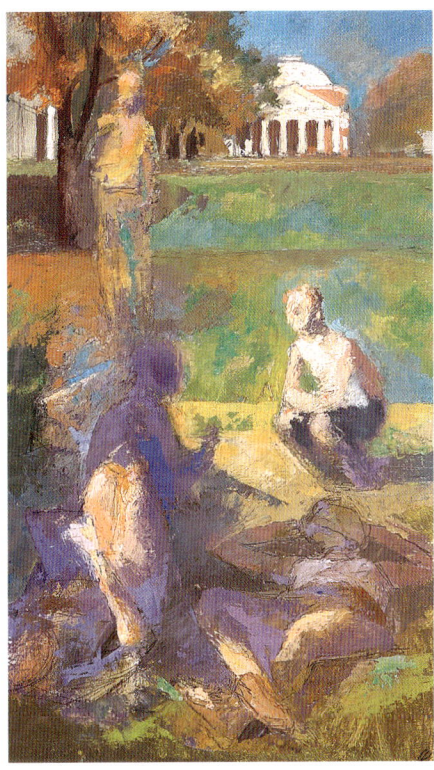
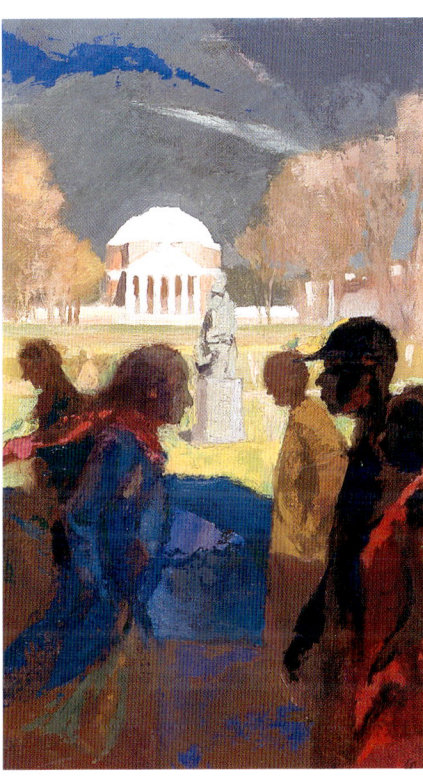

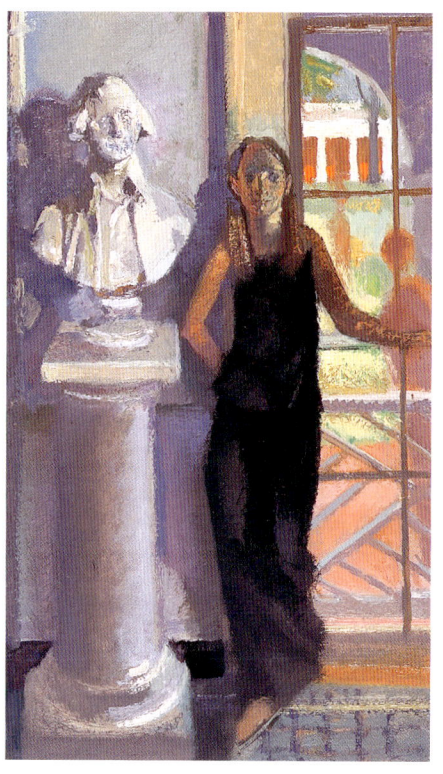 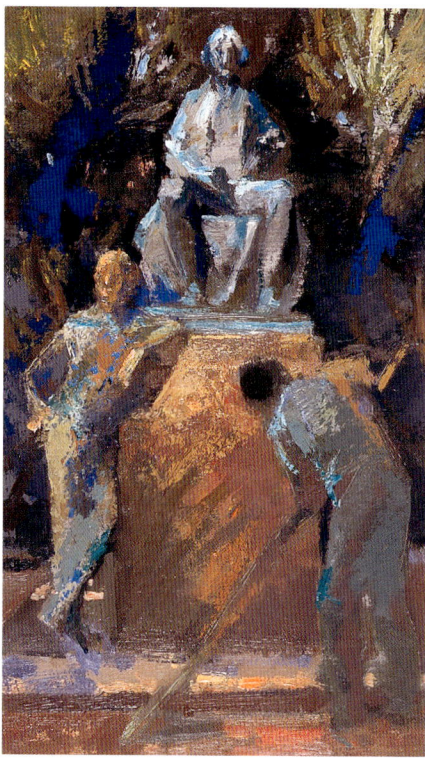 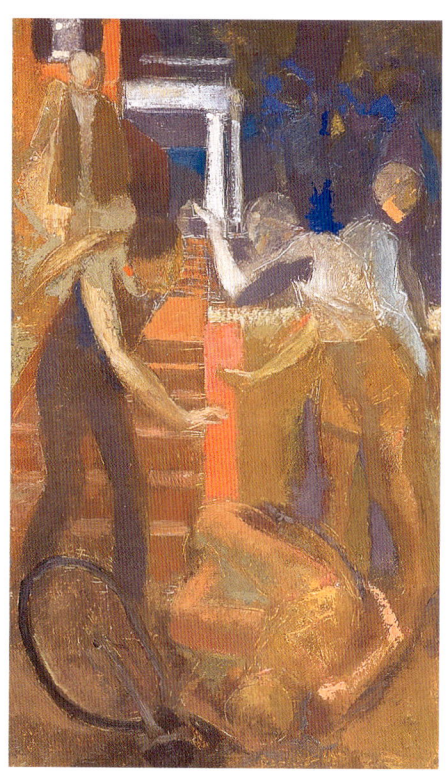

30

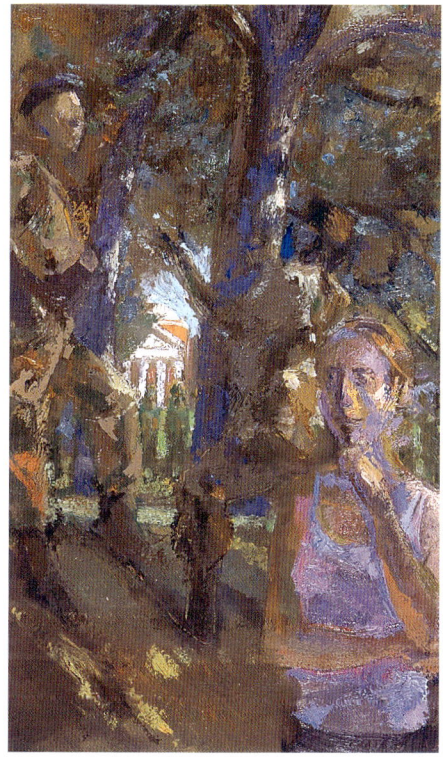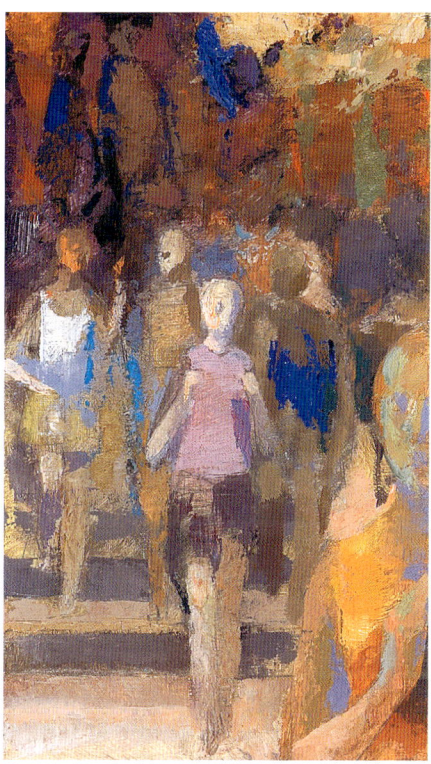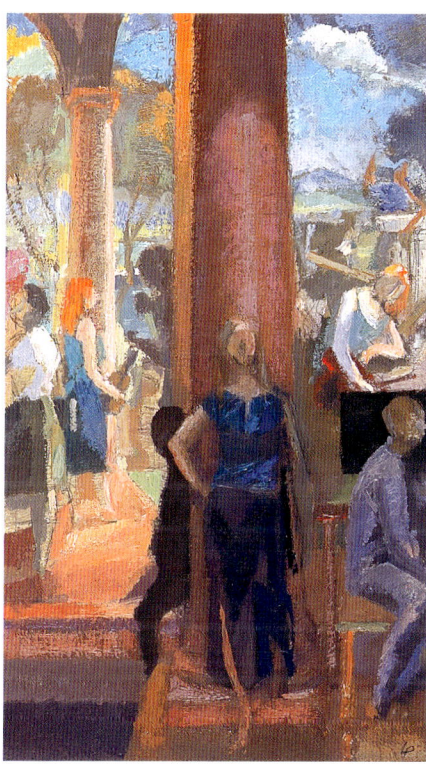

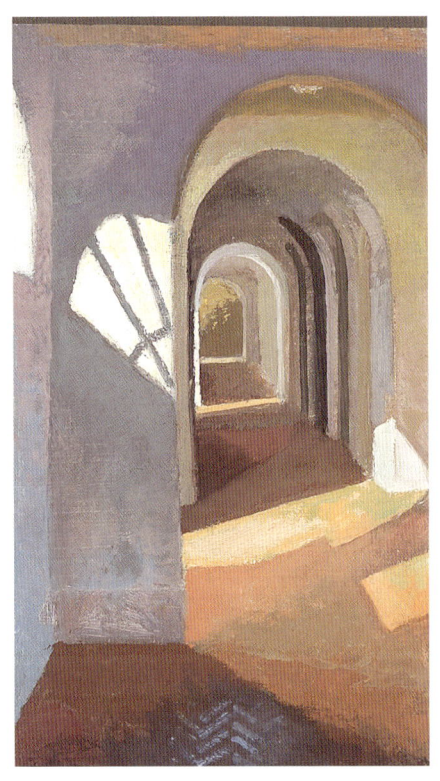 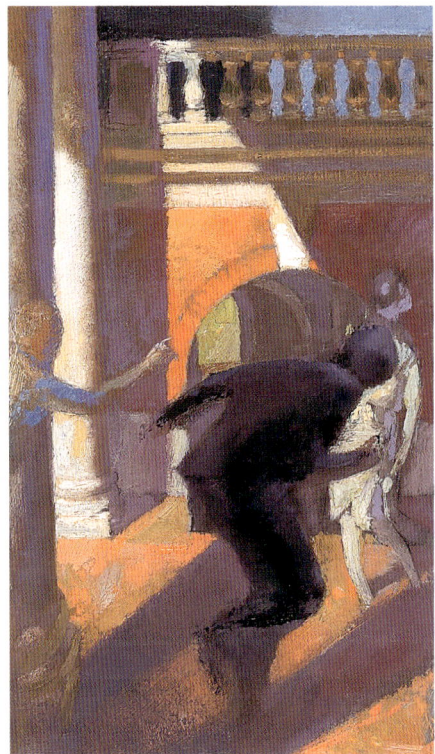 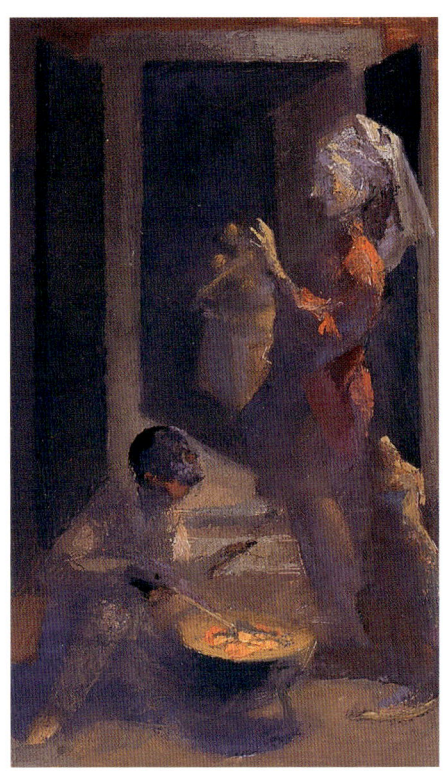

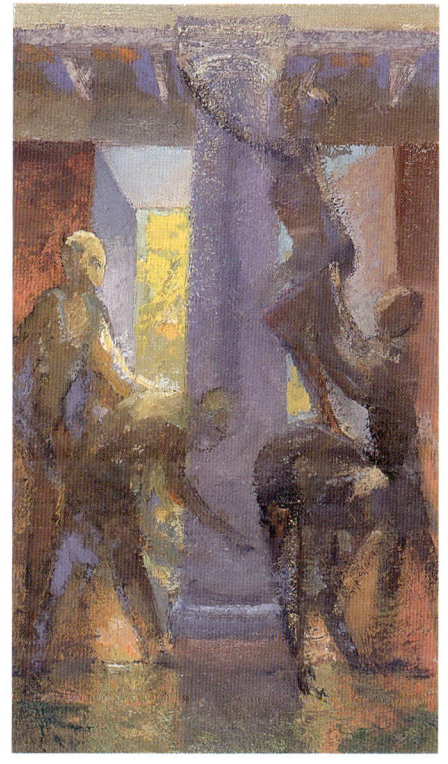 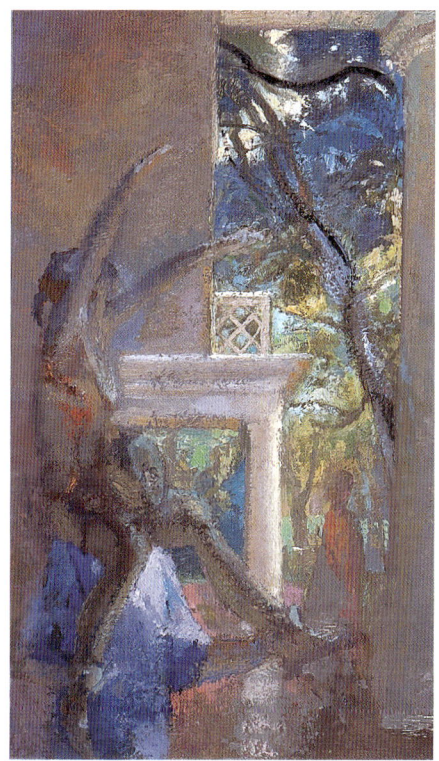 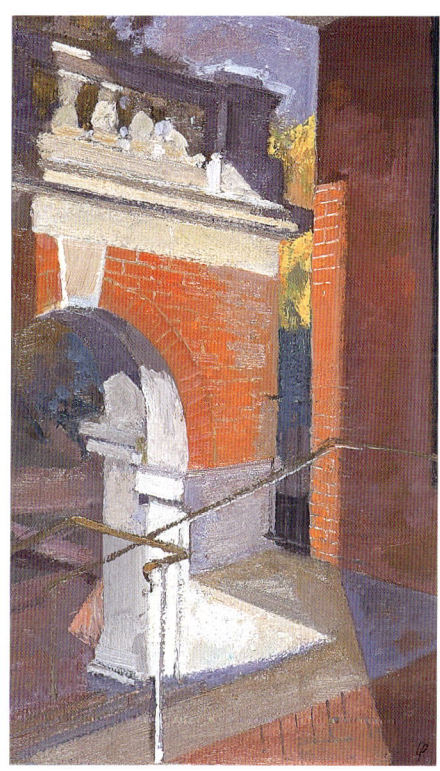

33

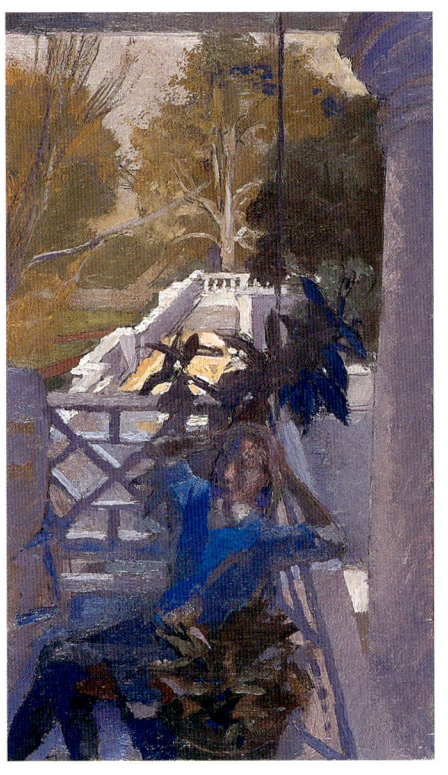
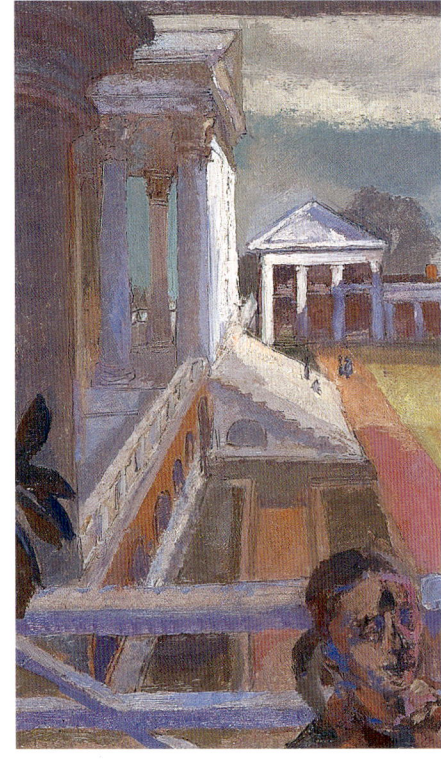
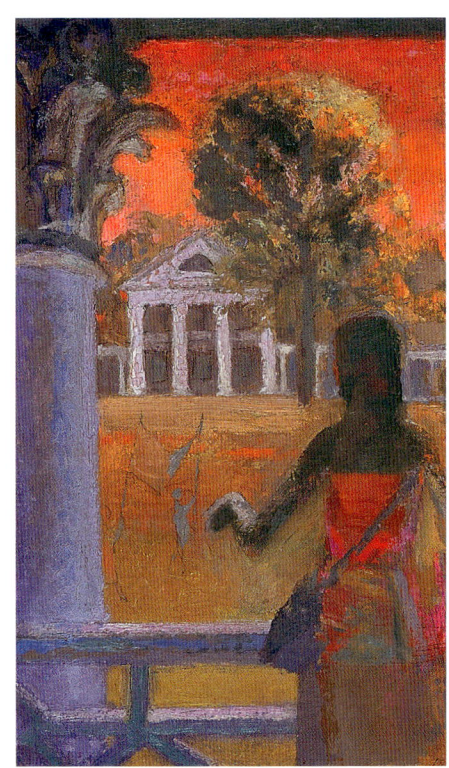

34

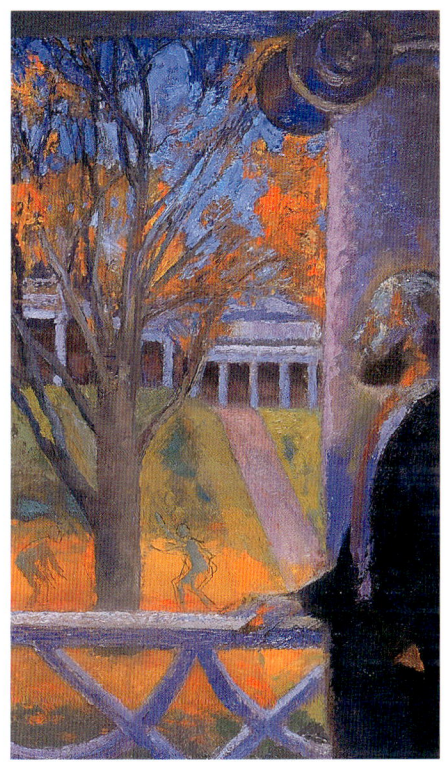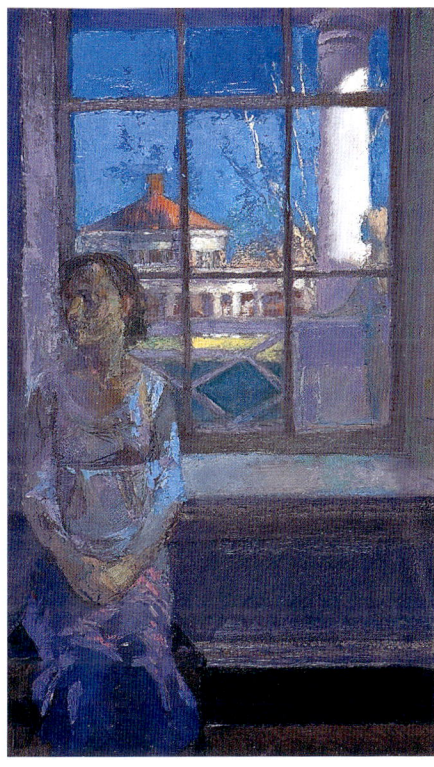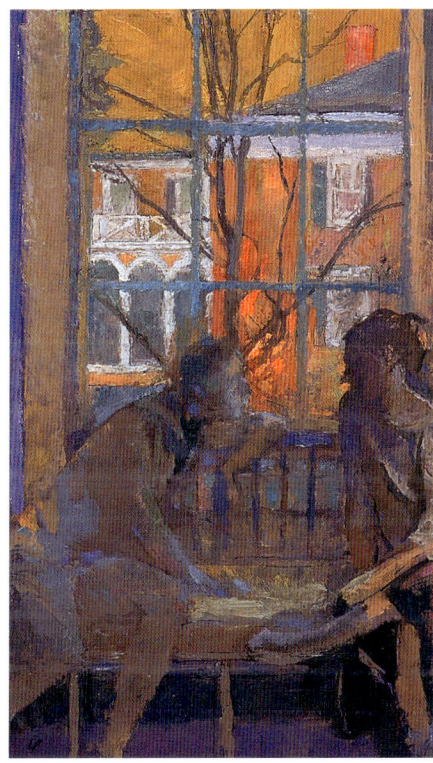

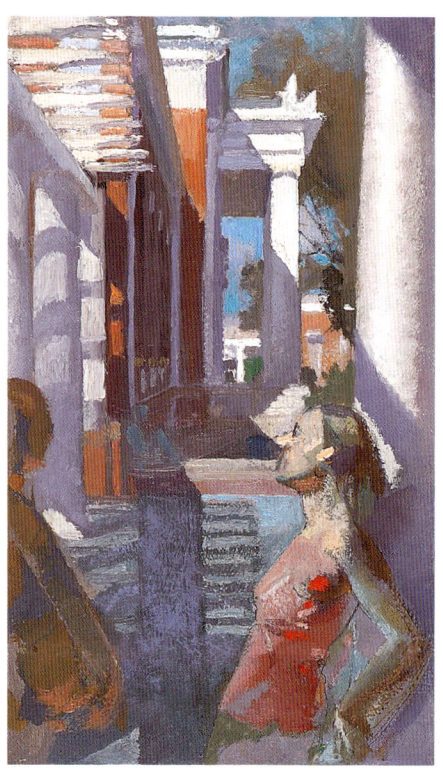 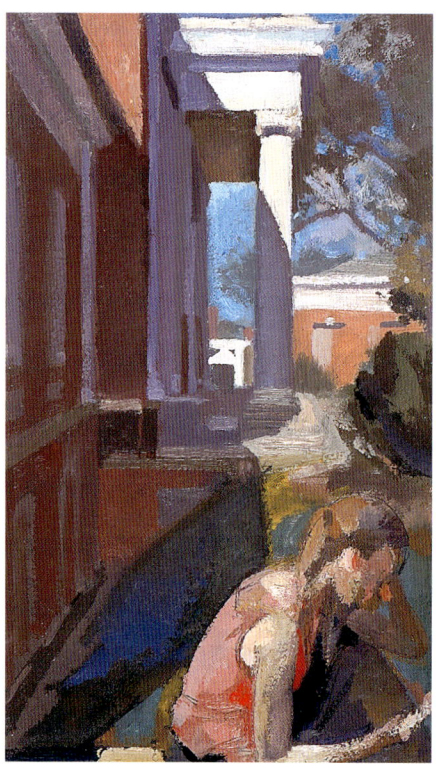 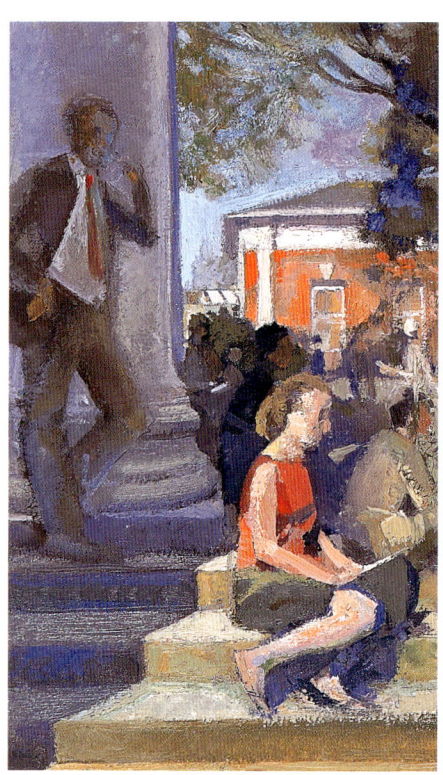

36

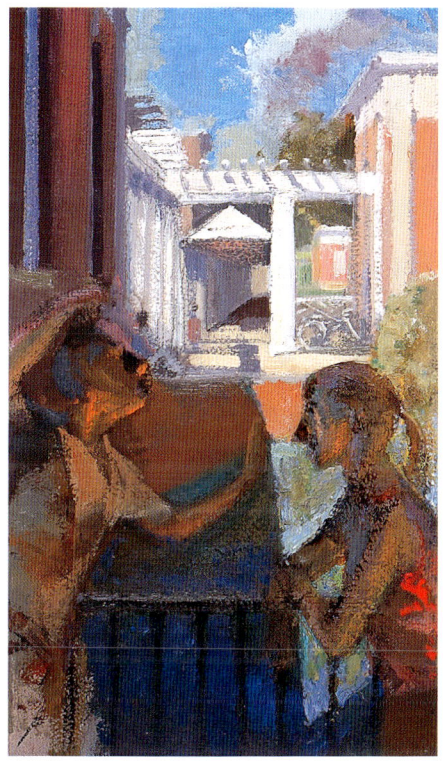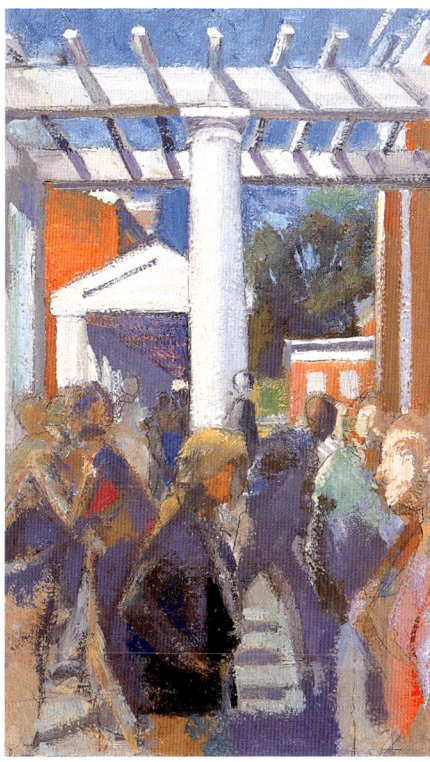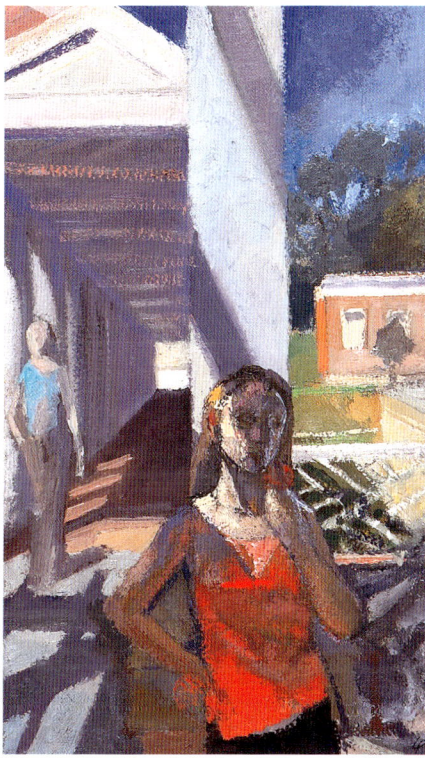

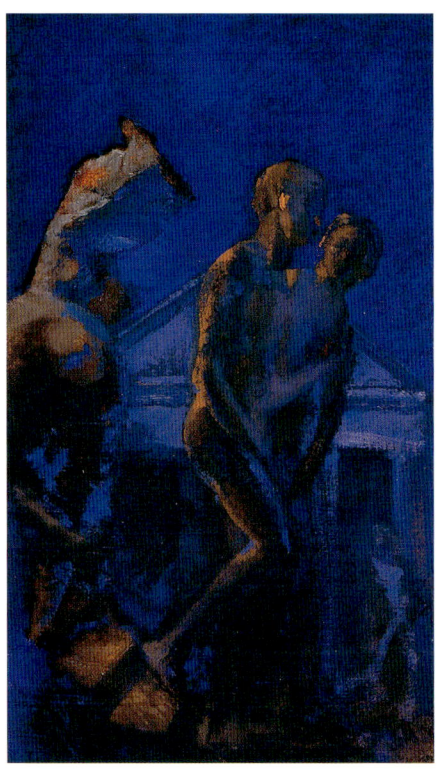 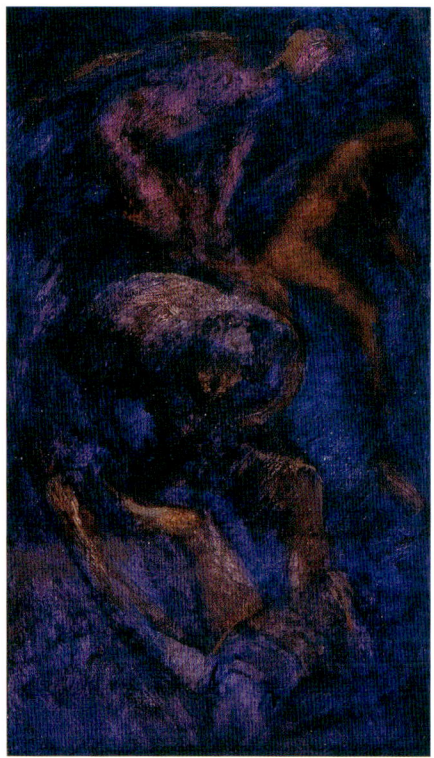 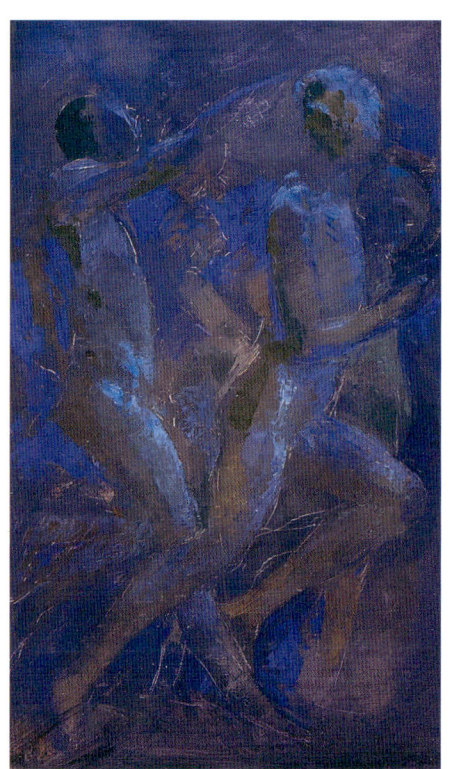

38

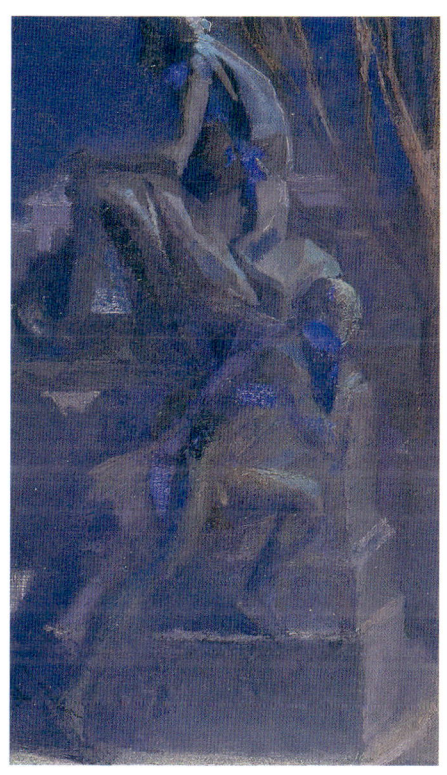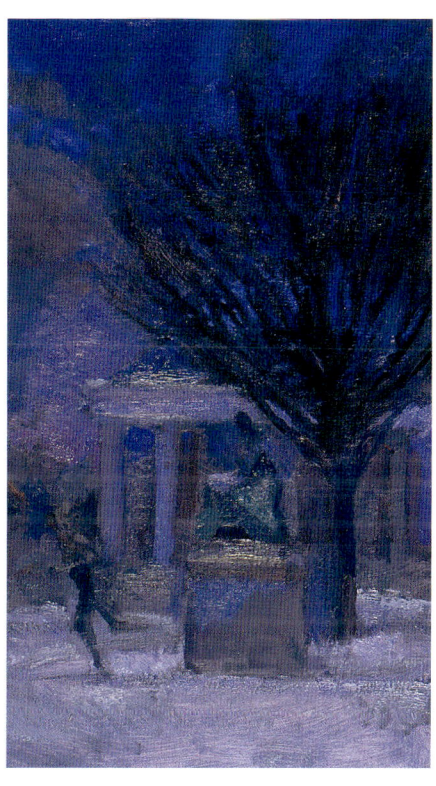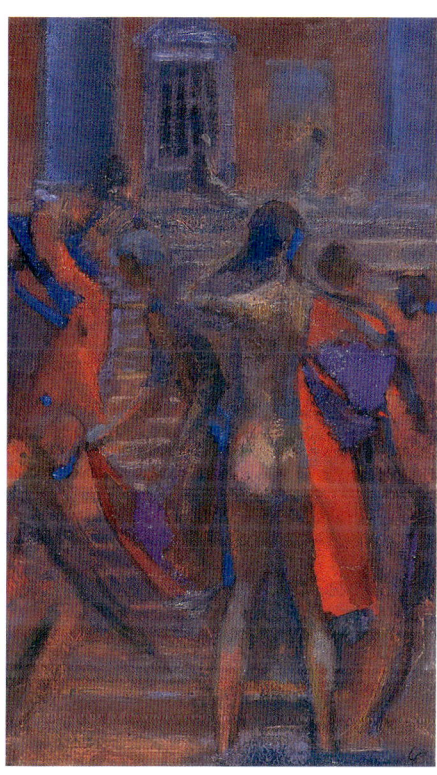

39

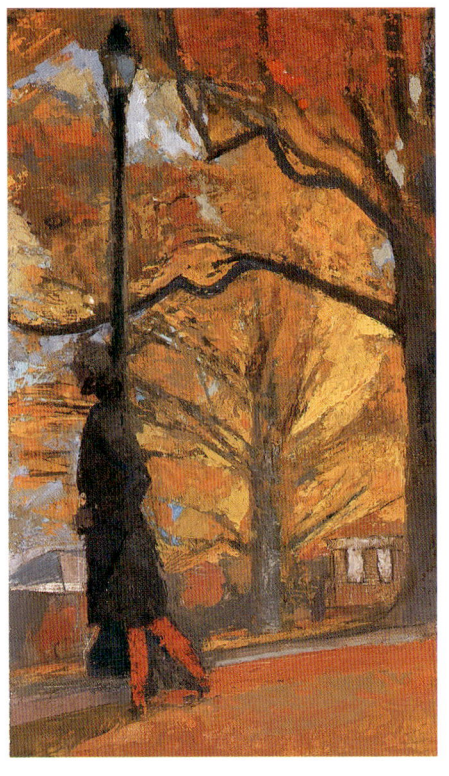 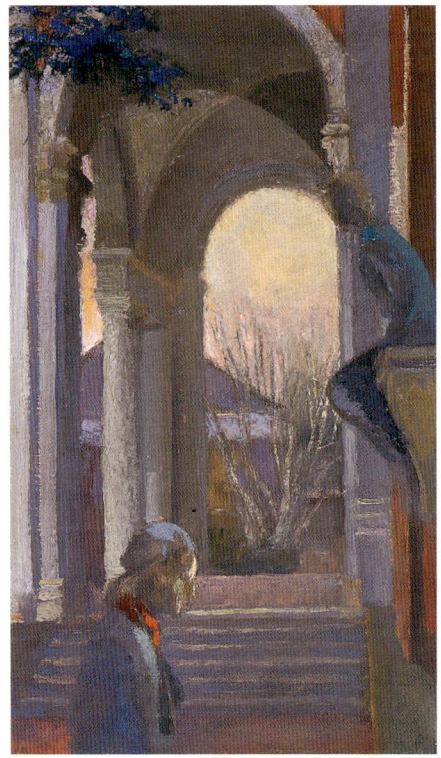 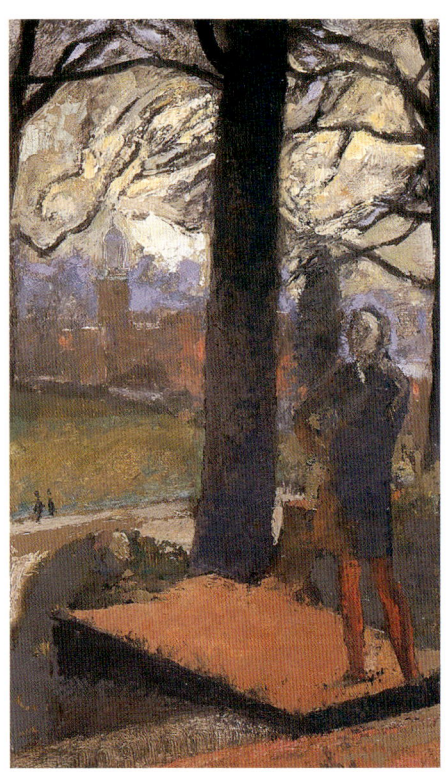

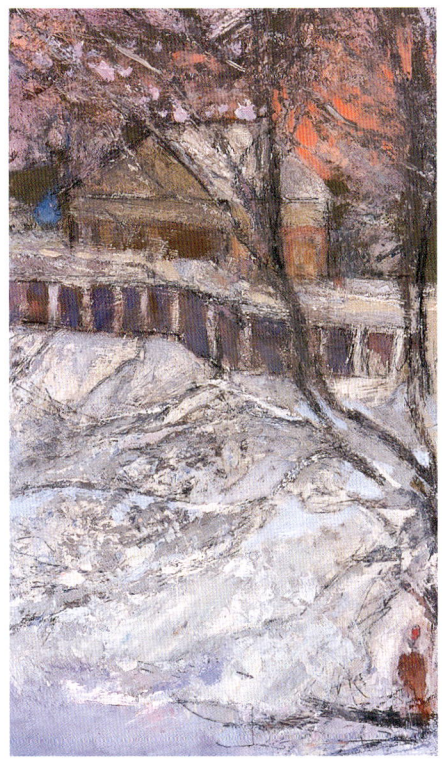 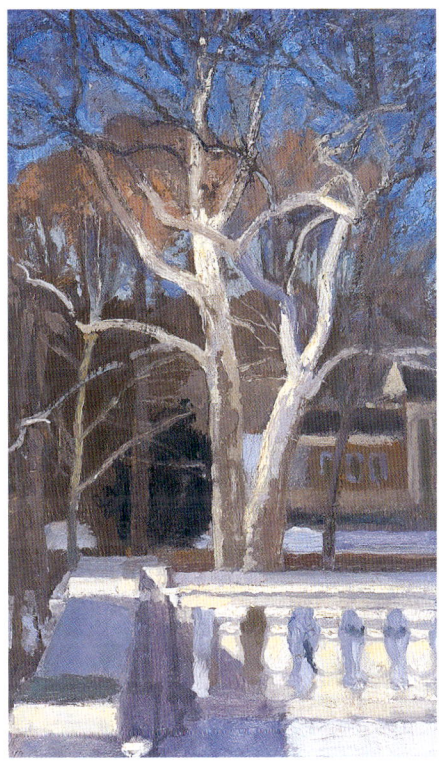 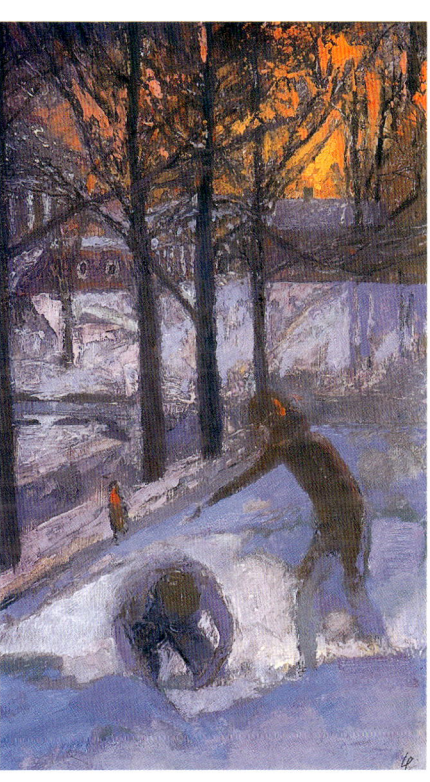

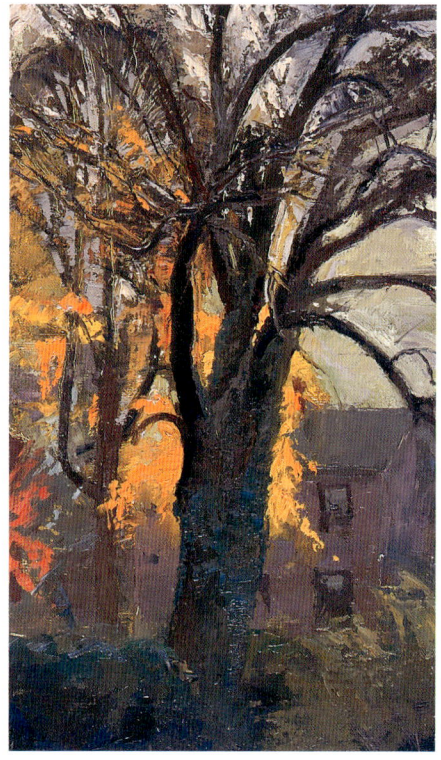 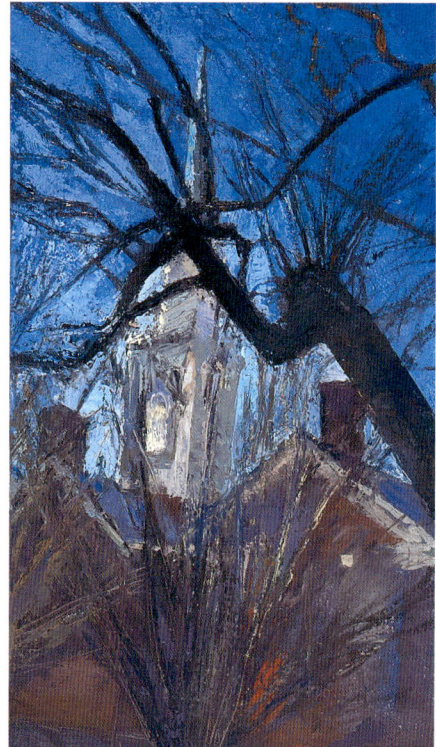 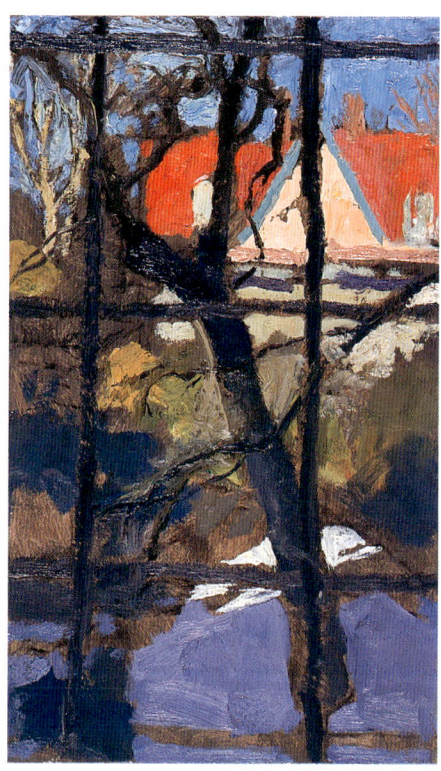

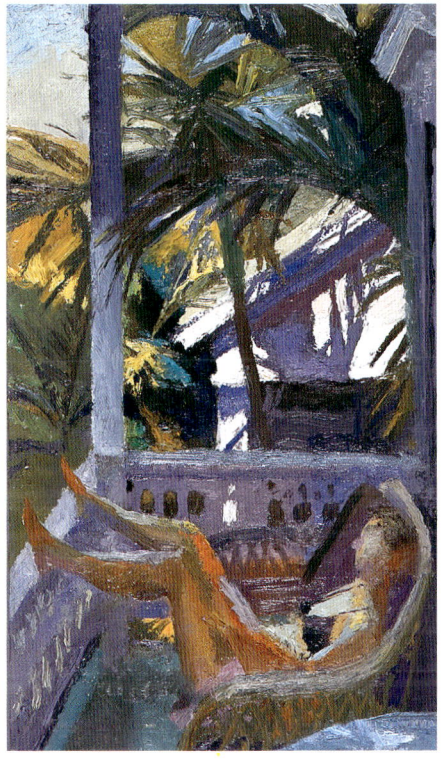
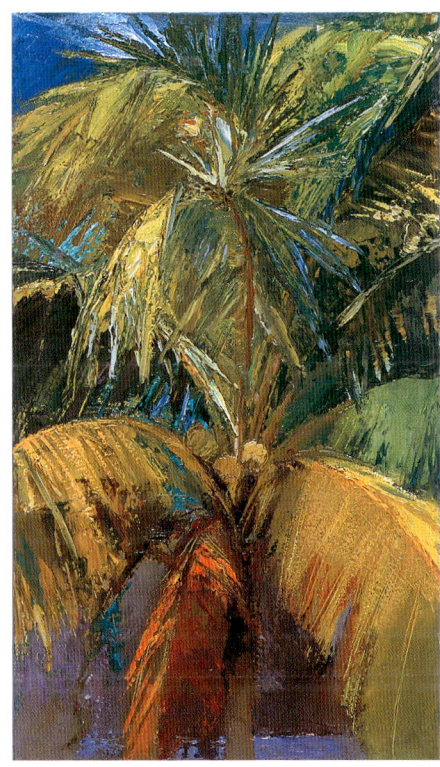
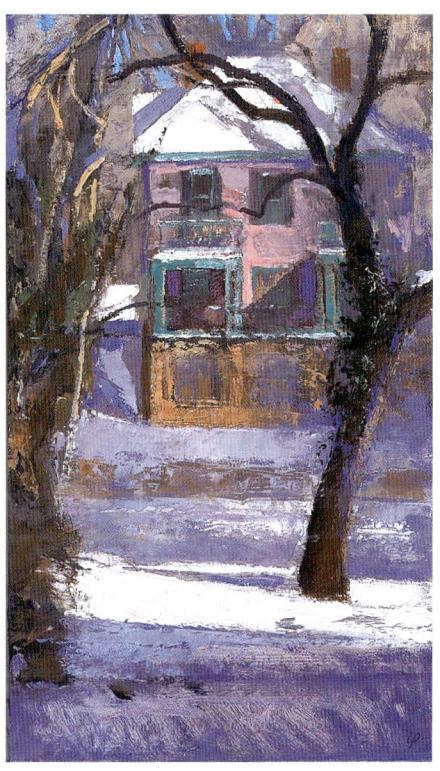

43

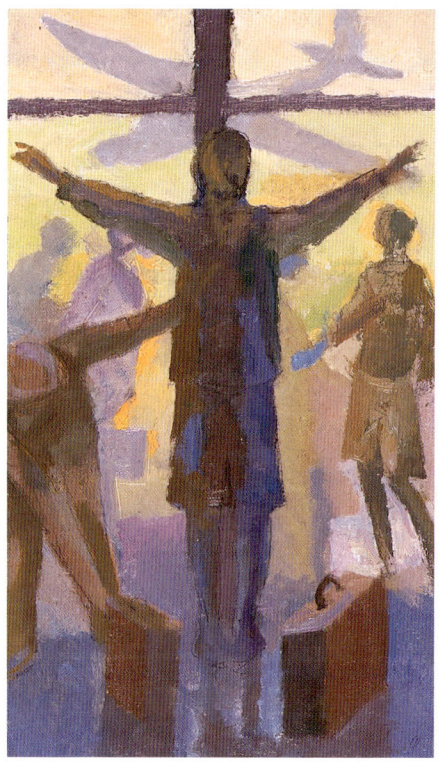 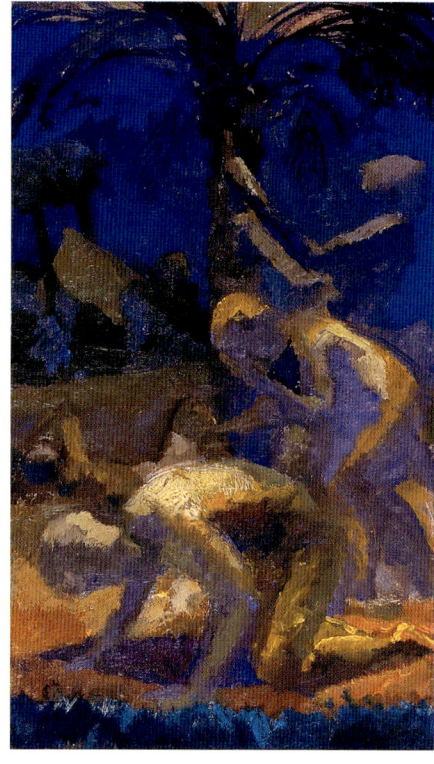 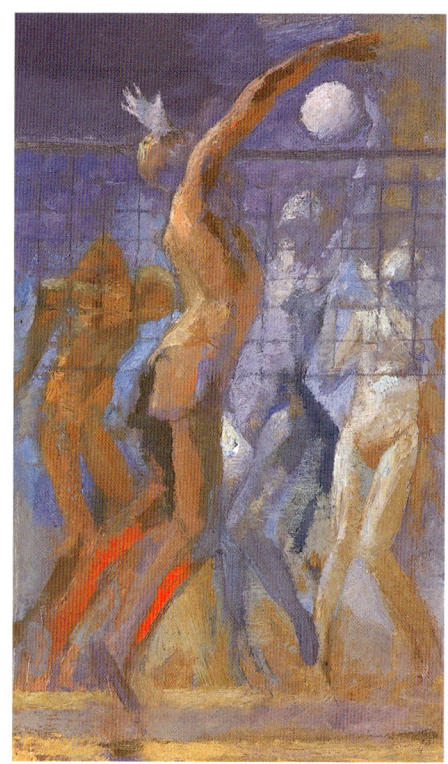

44

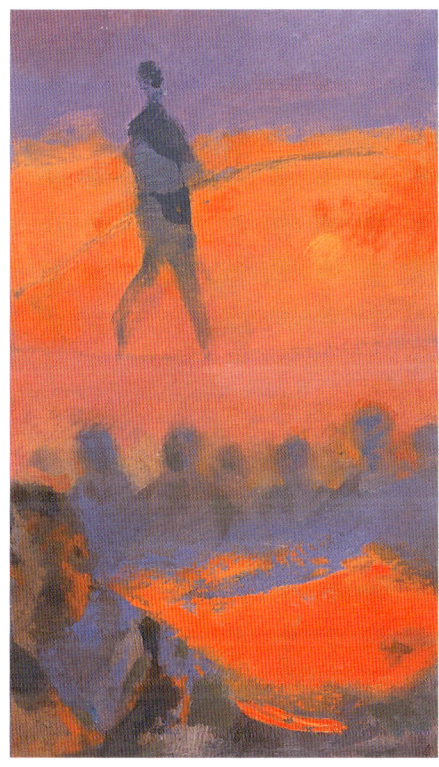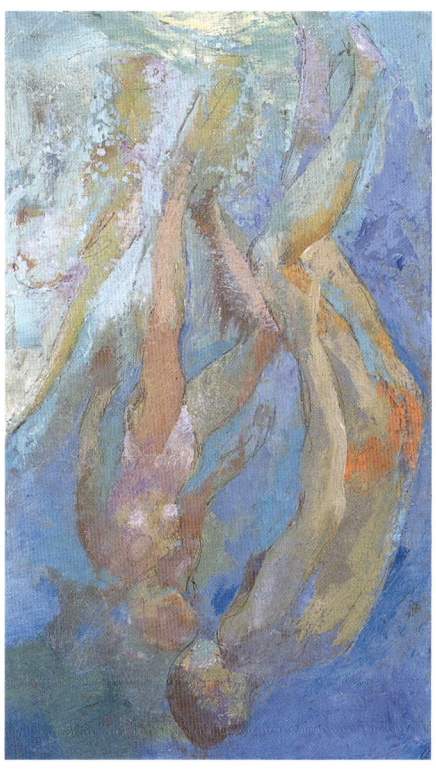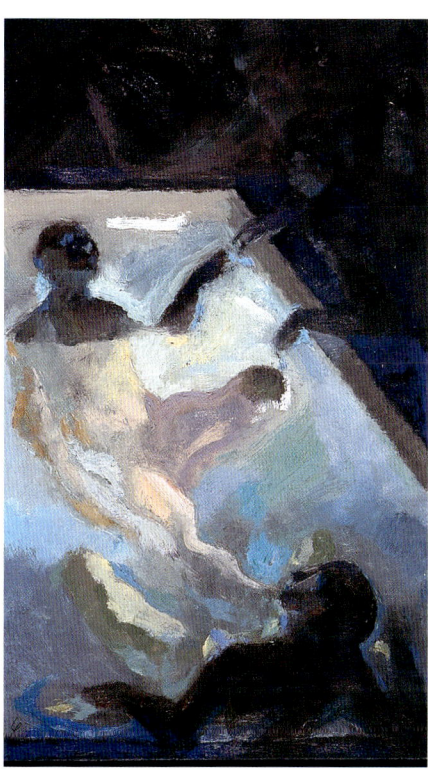

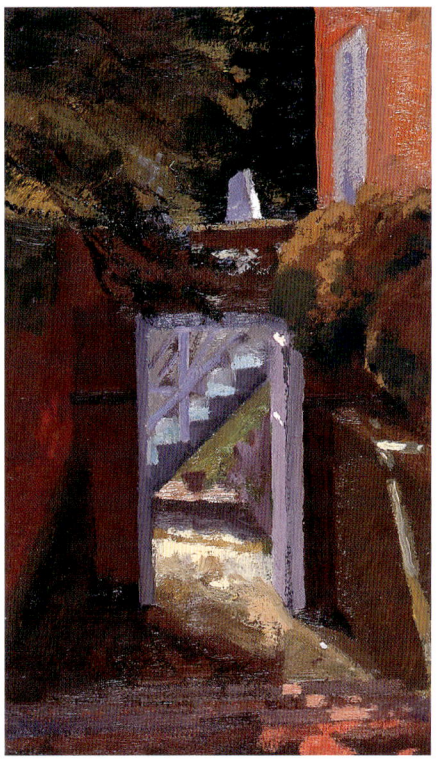 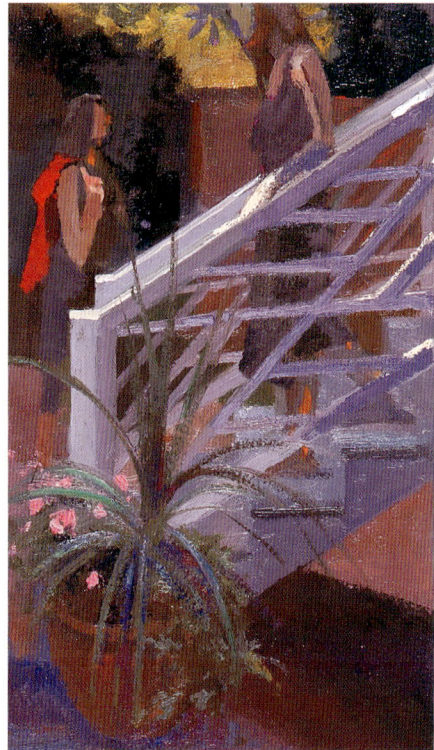 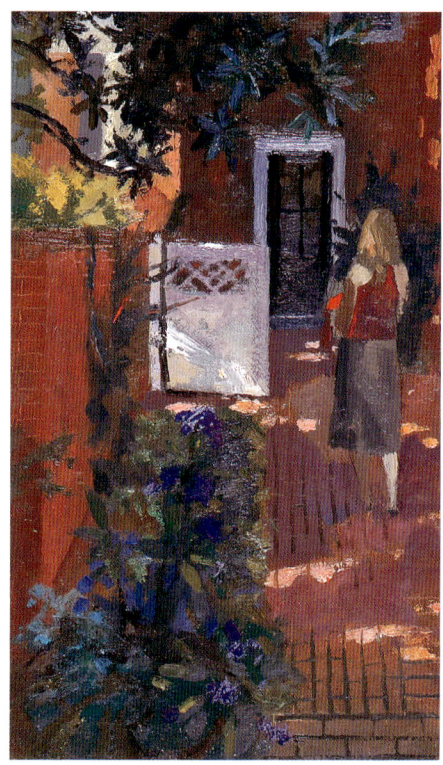

46

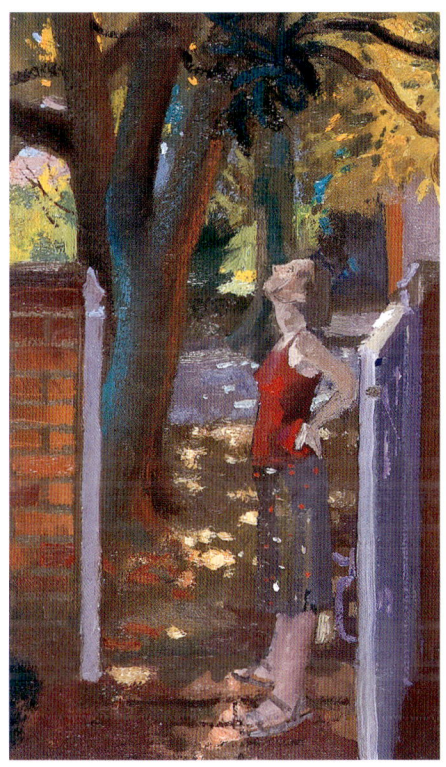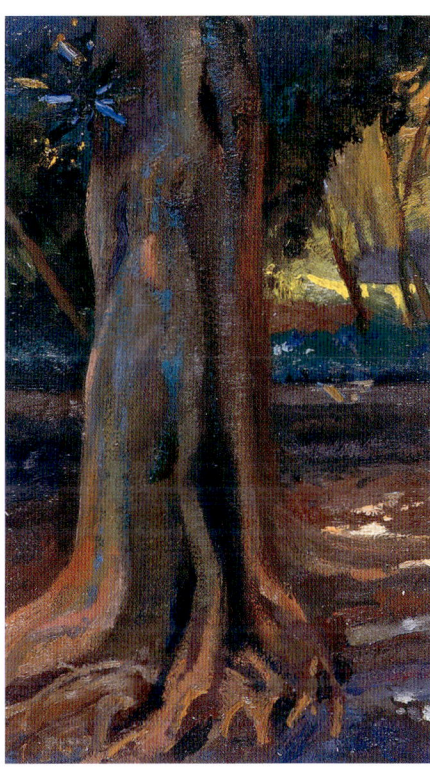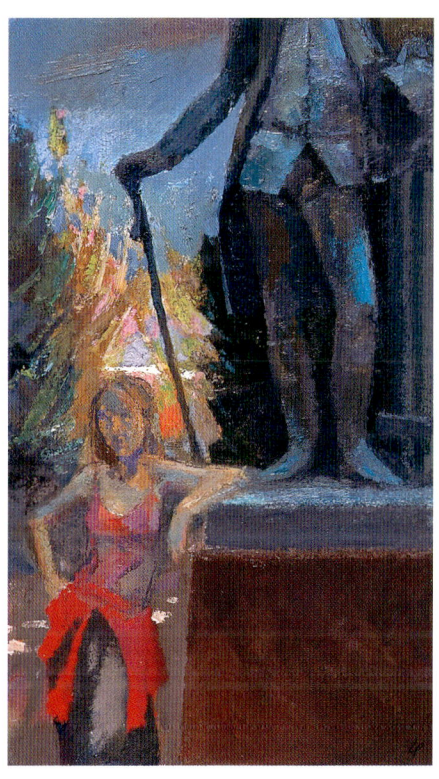

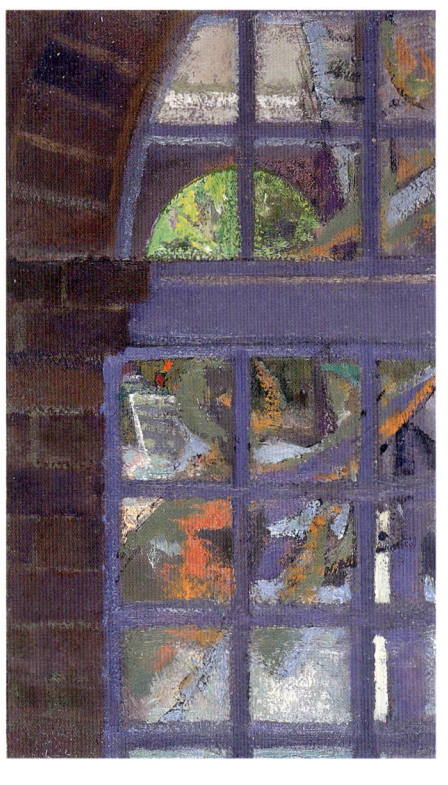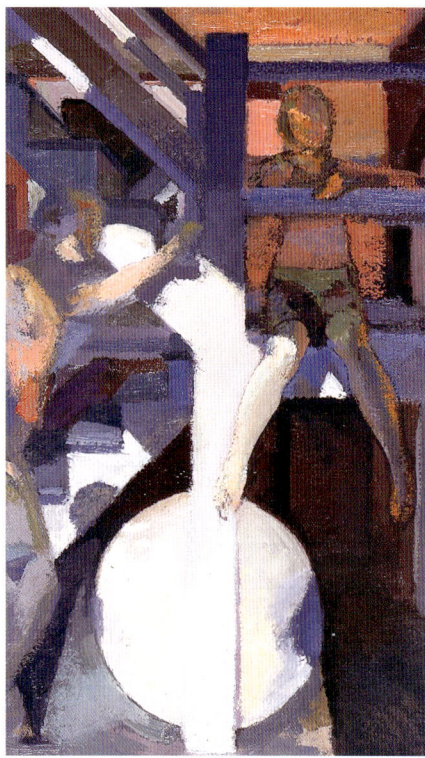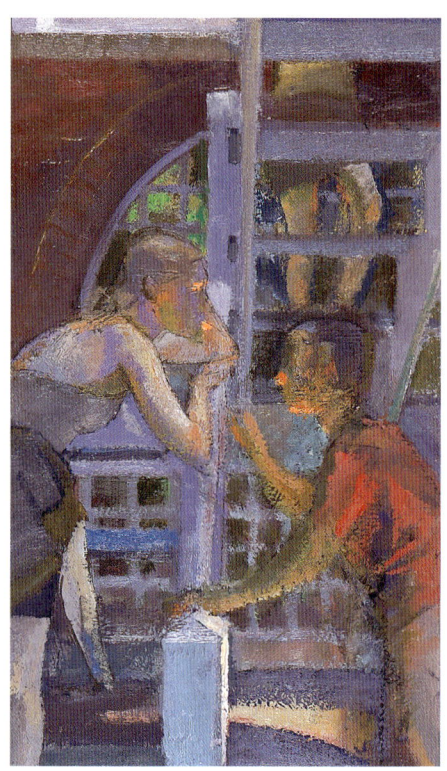

48

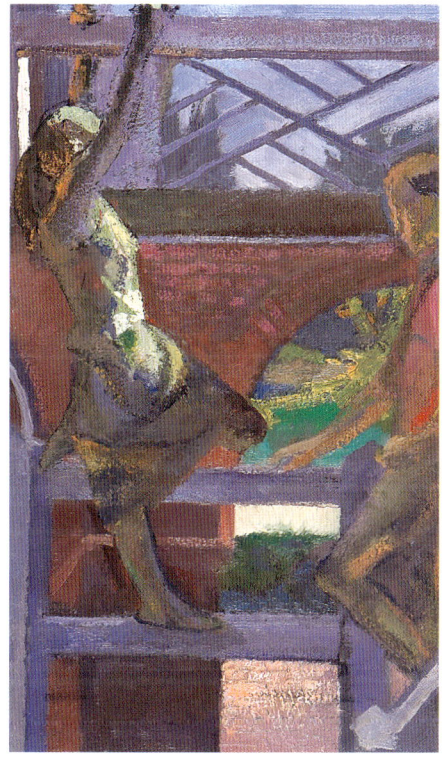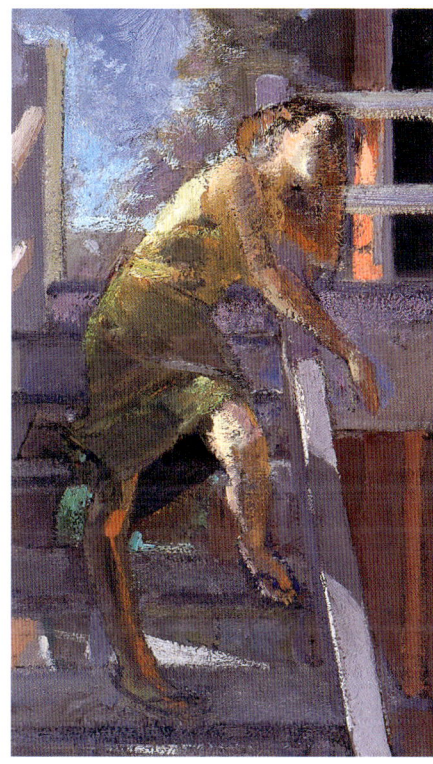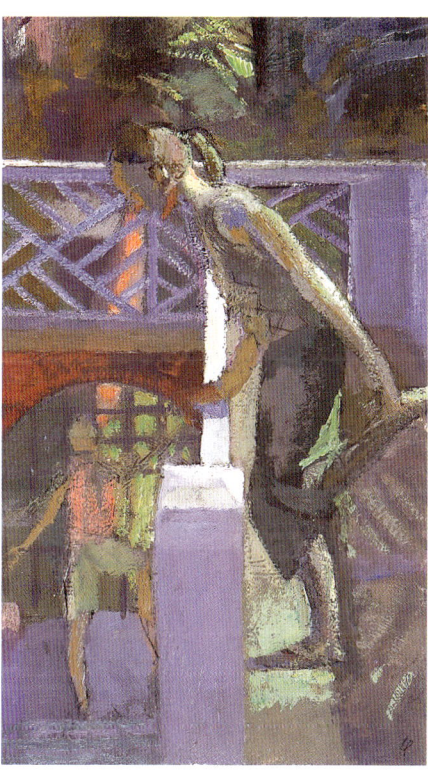

49

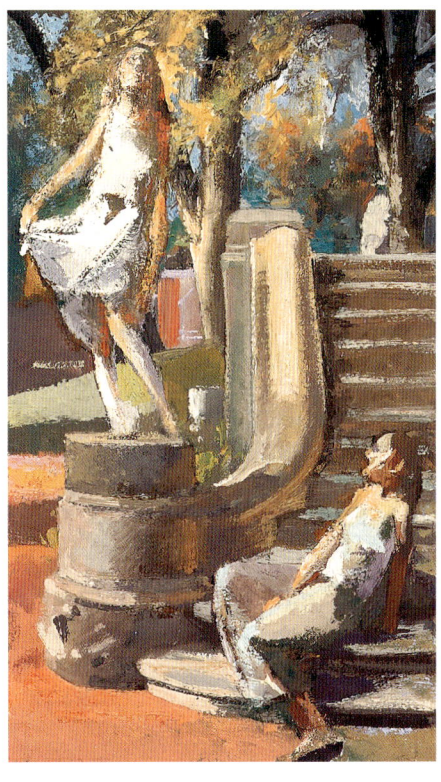
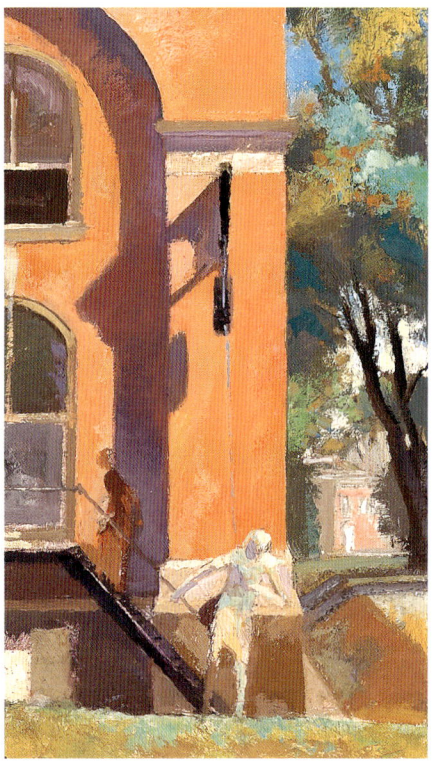
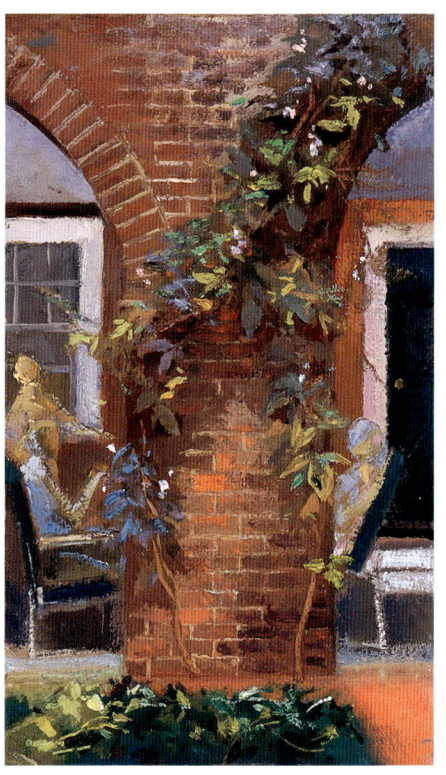

50

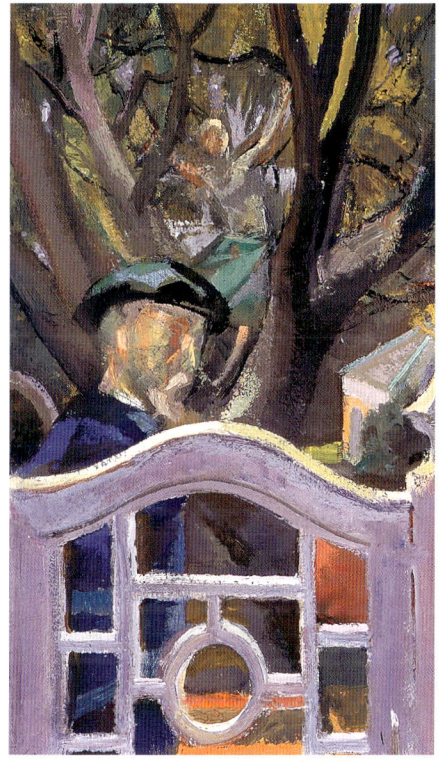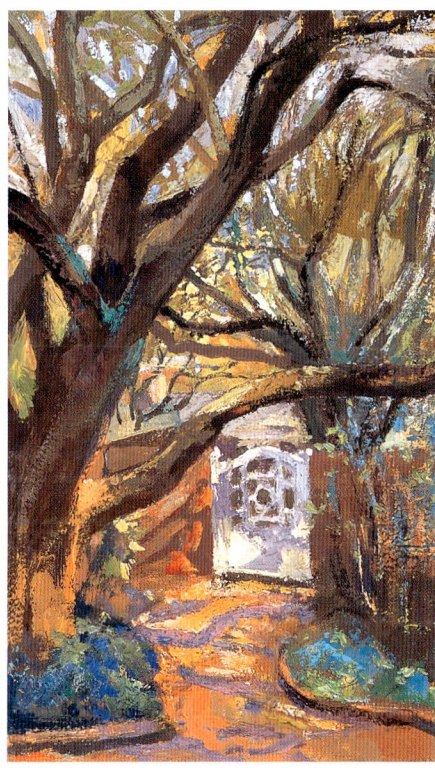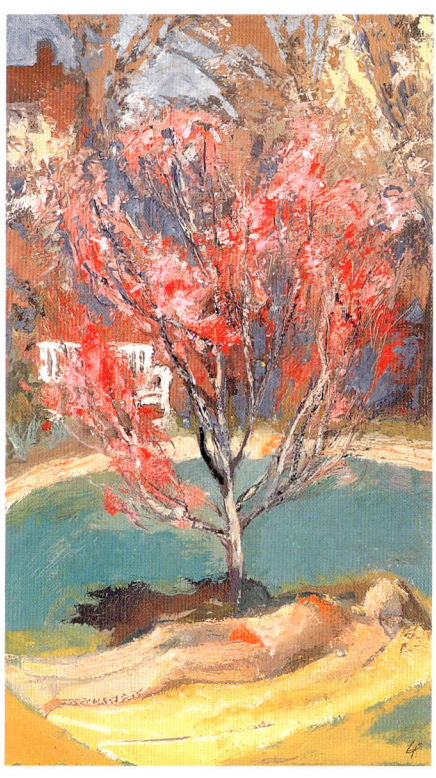

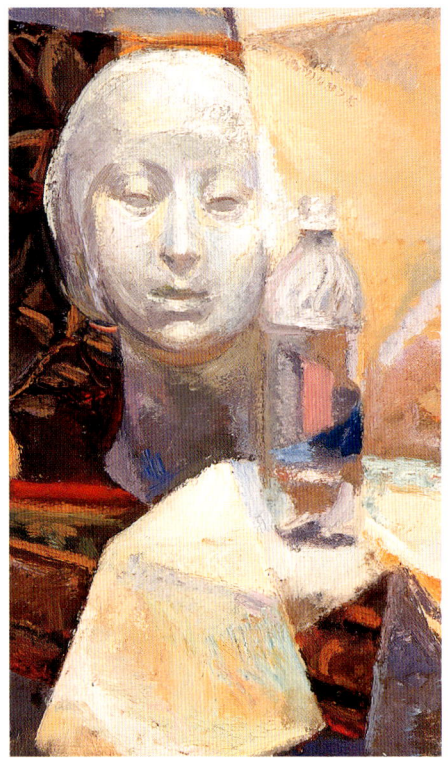
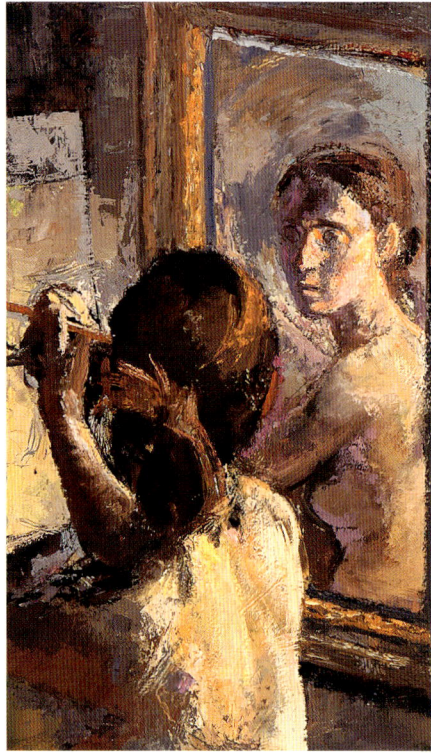
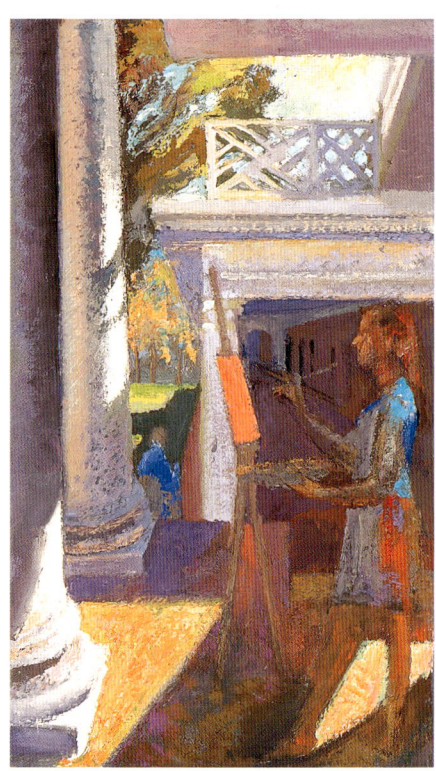

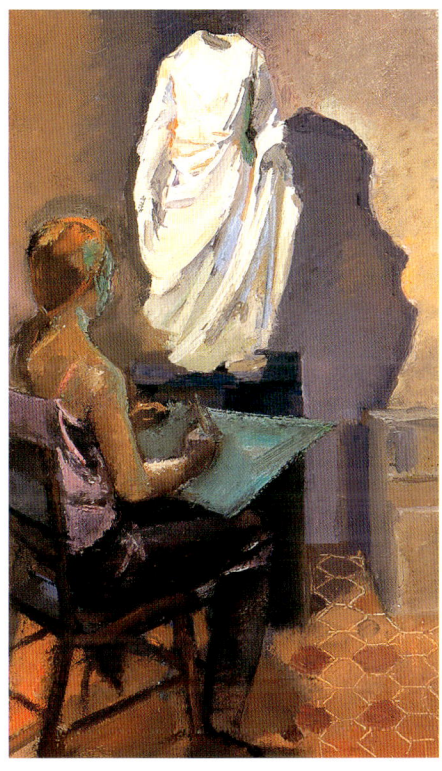
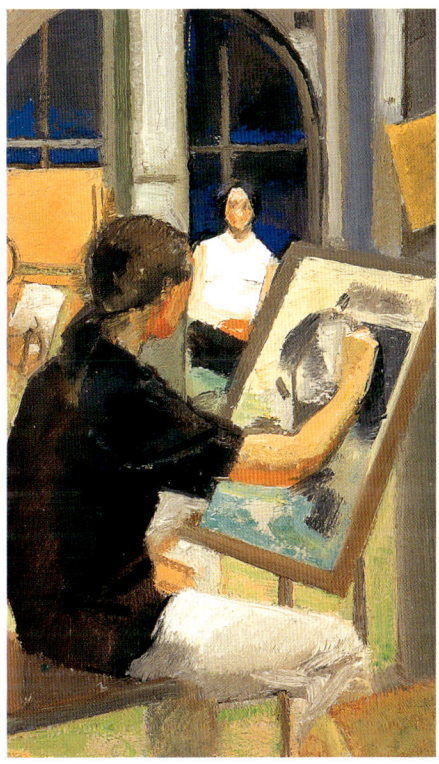
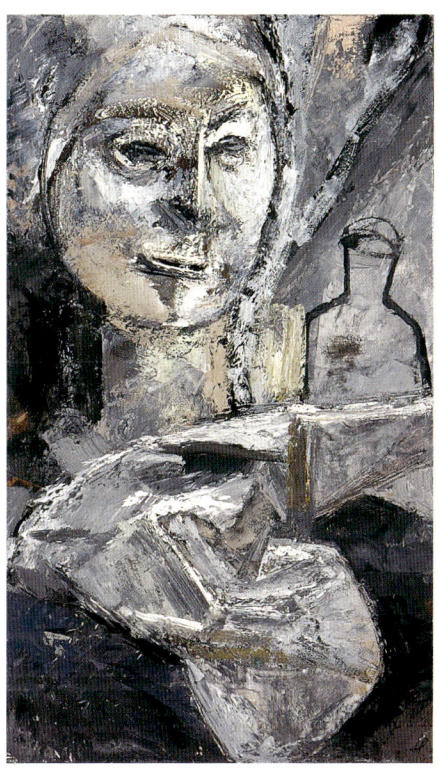

53

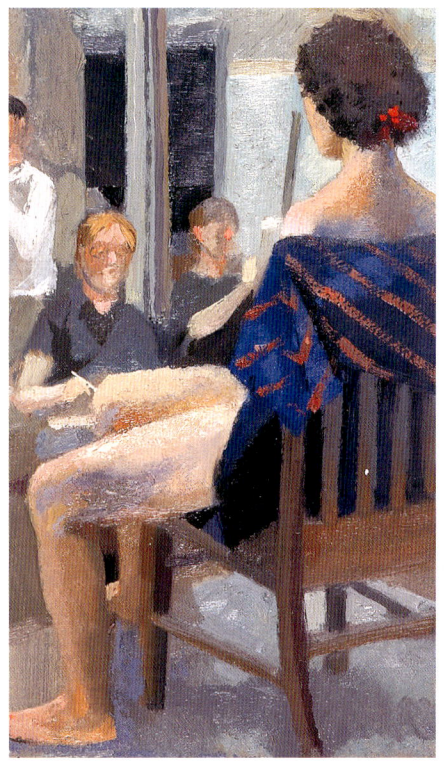 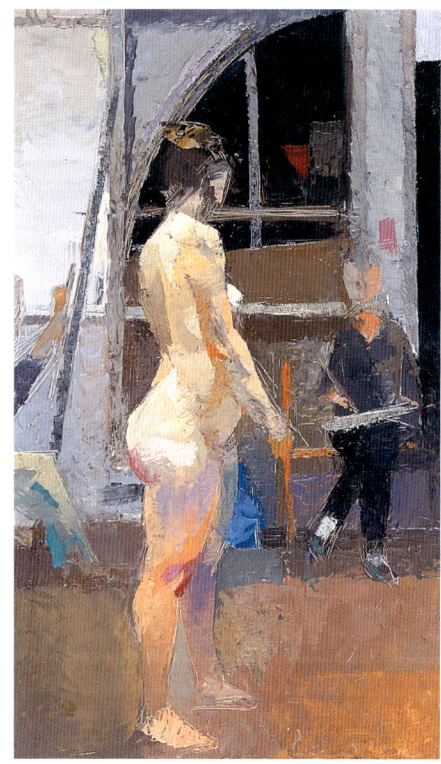 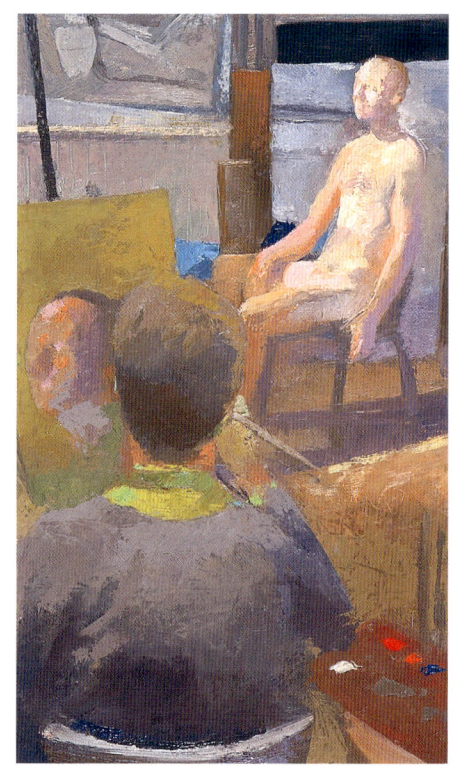

54

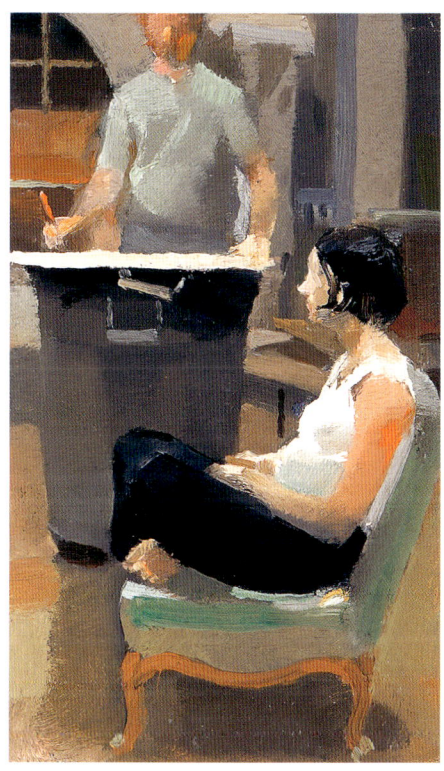 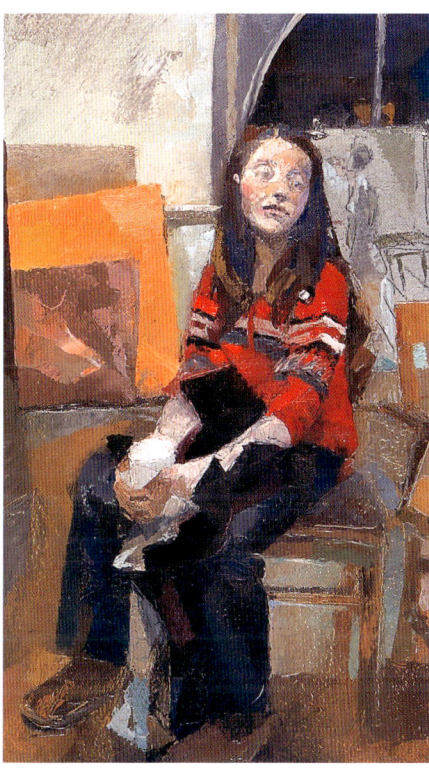 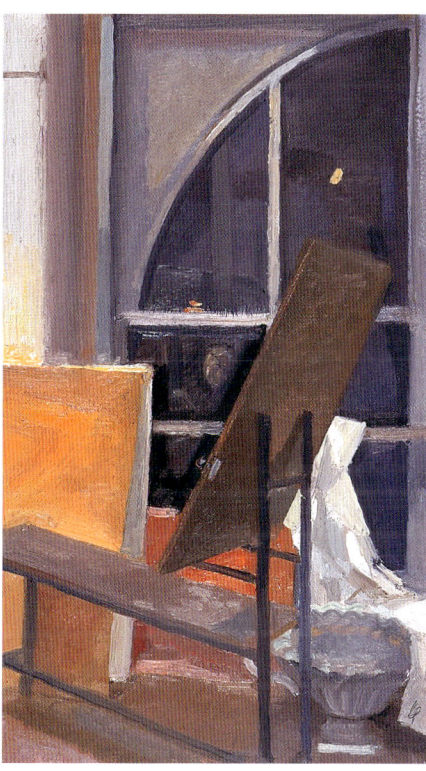

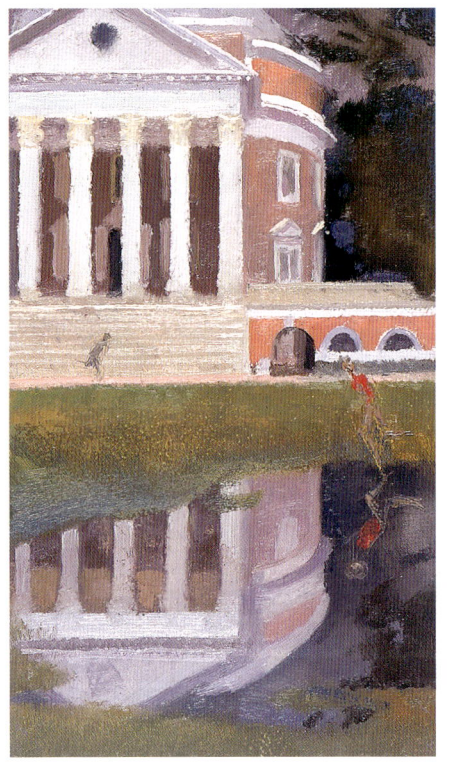
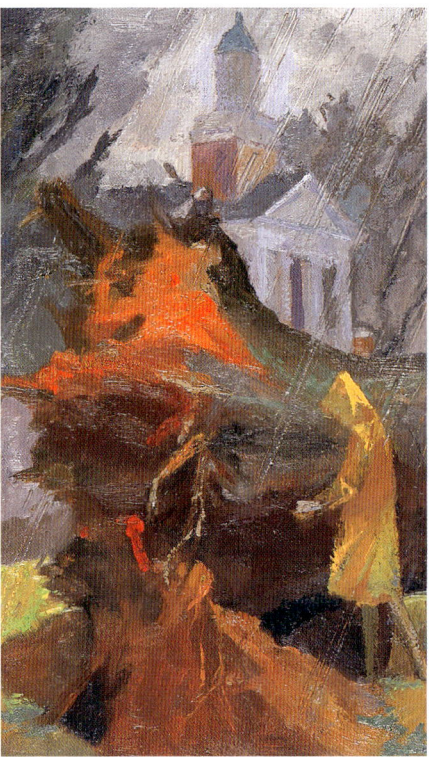
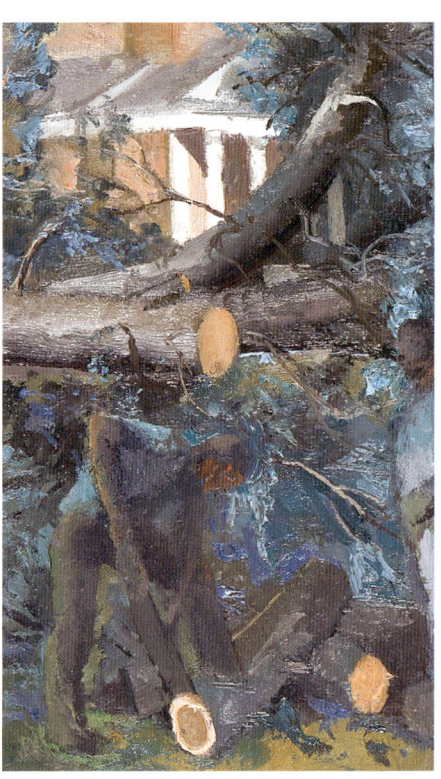

56

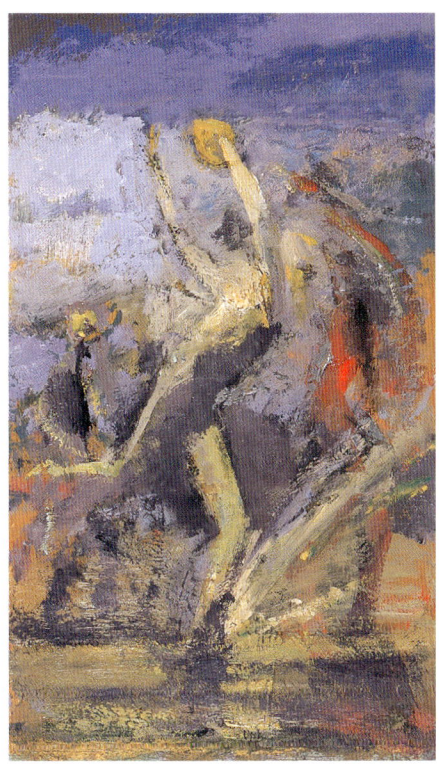
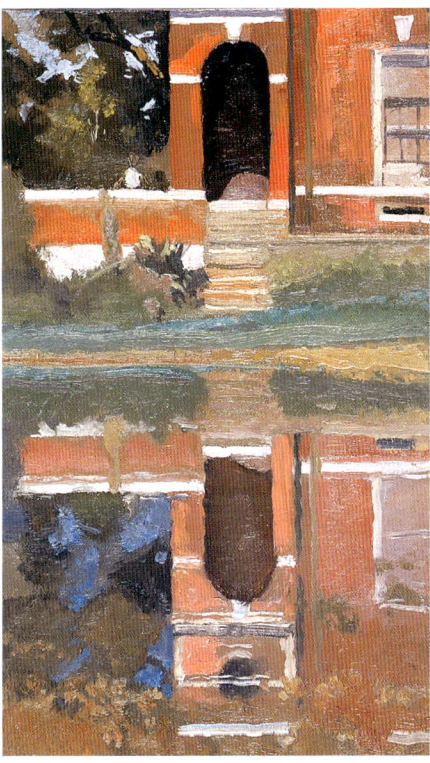
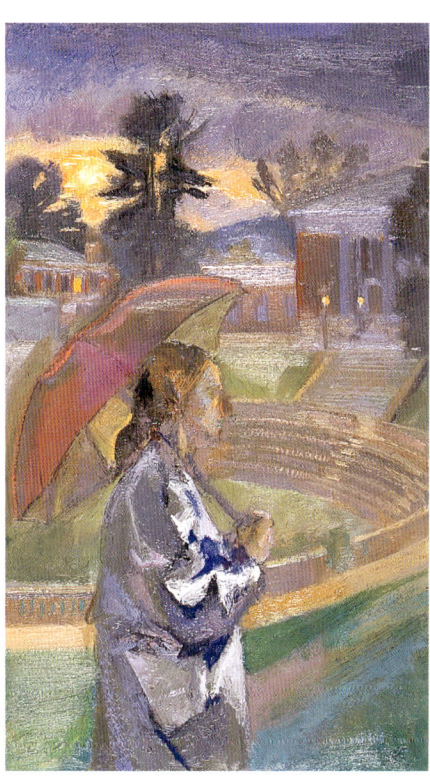

57

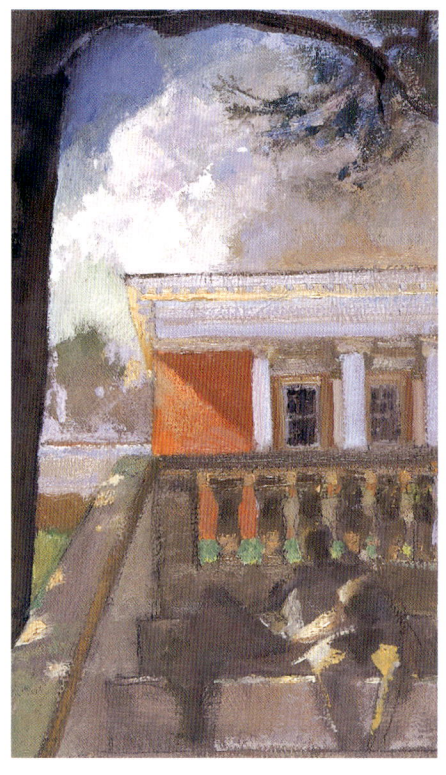 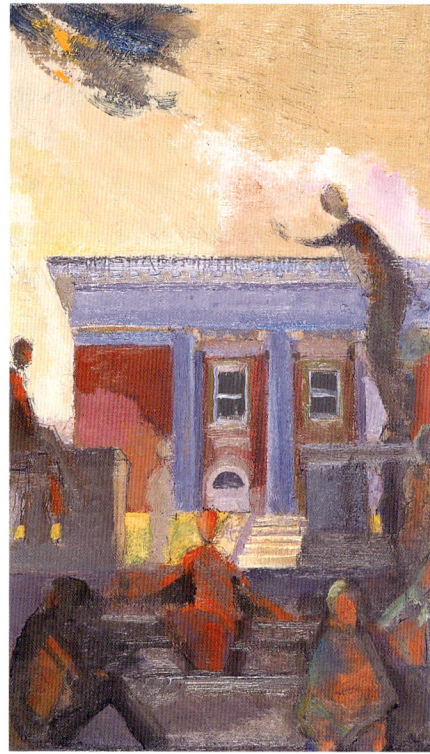 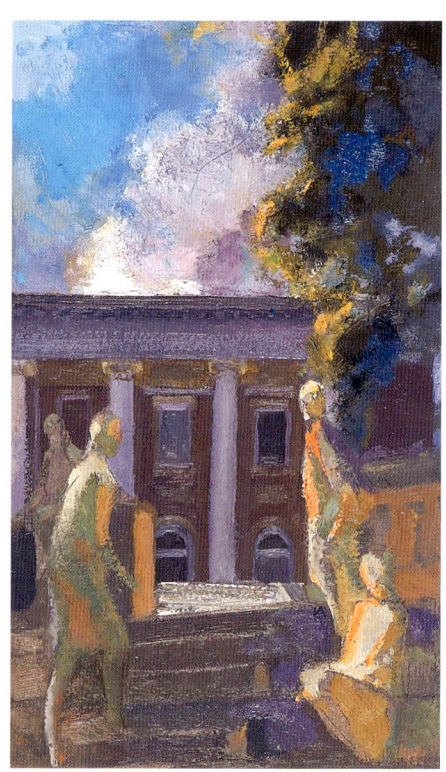

58

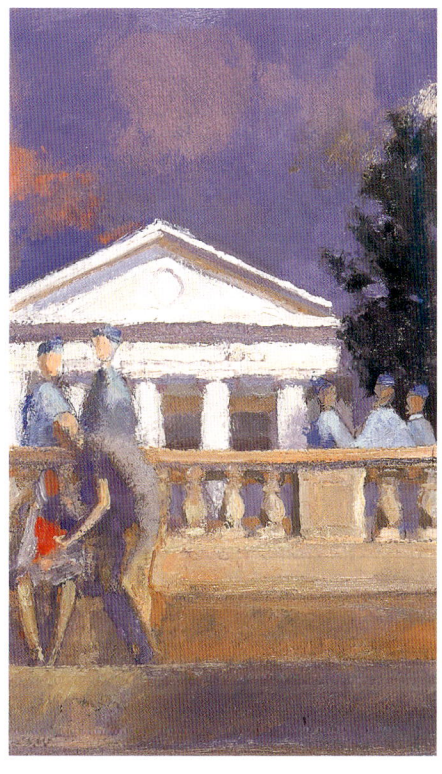 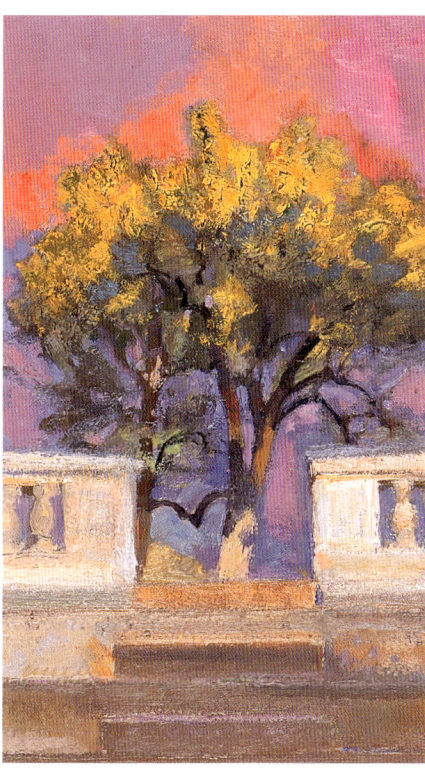 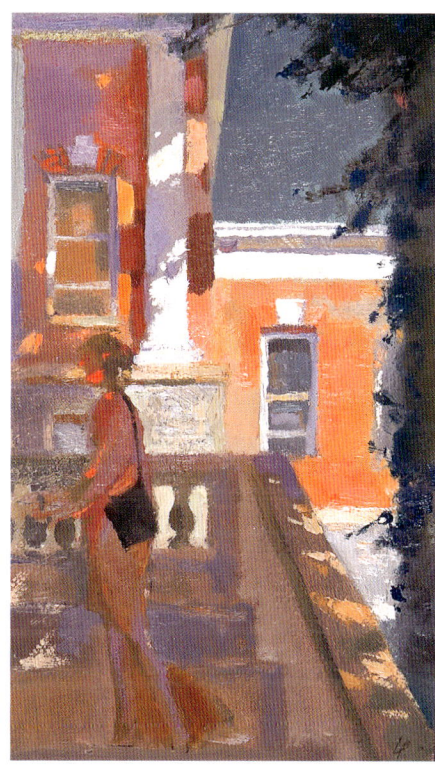

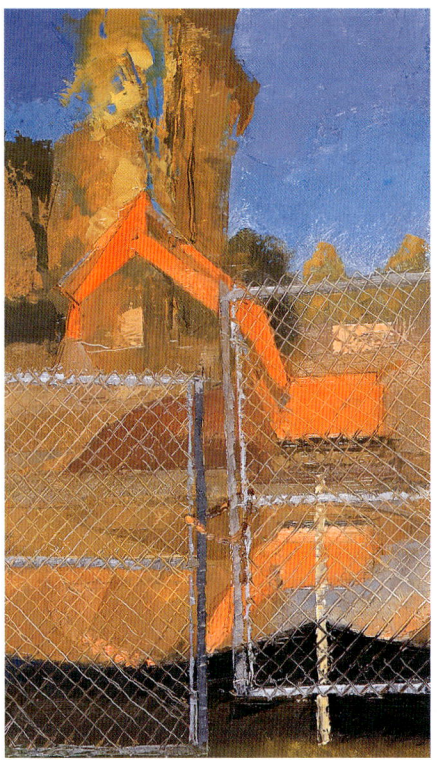 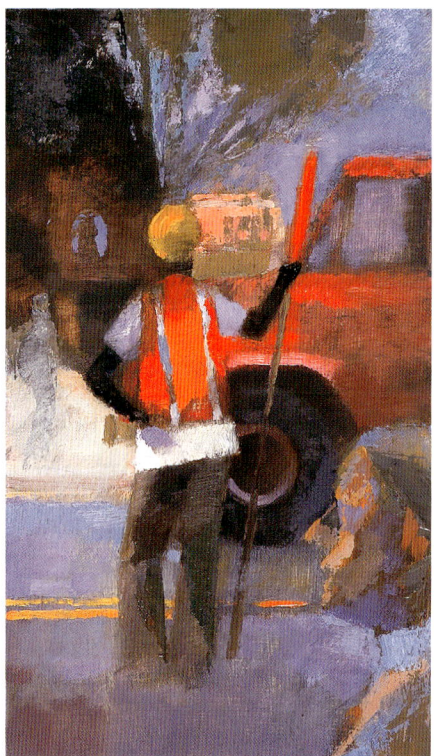 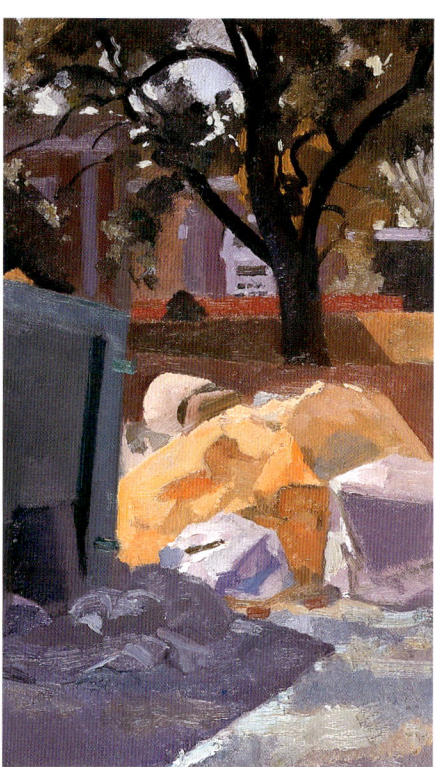

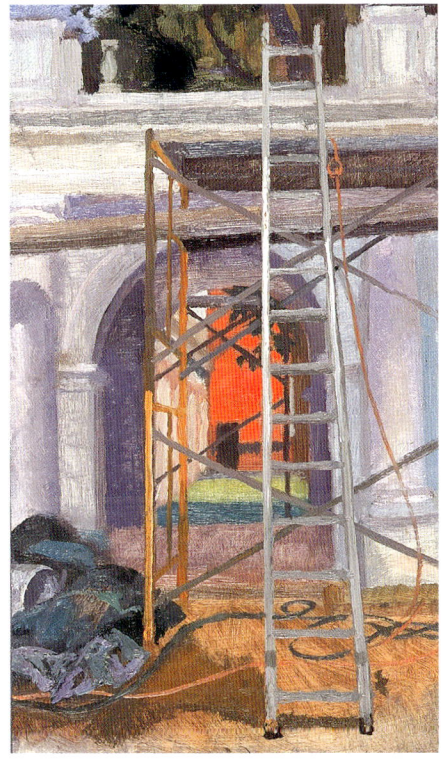 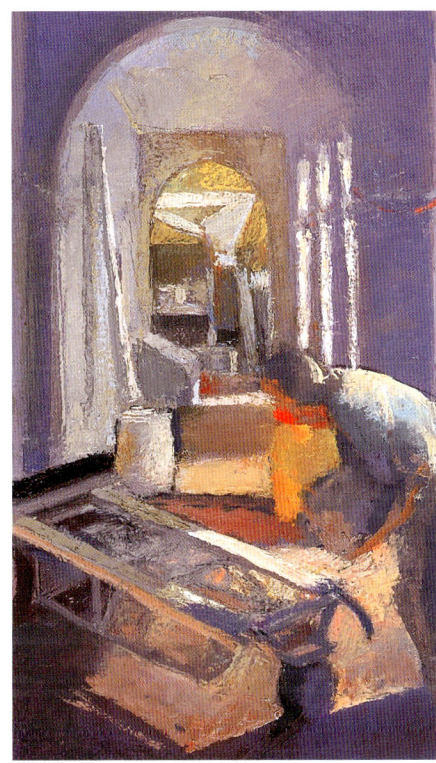 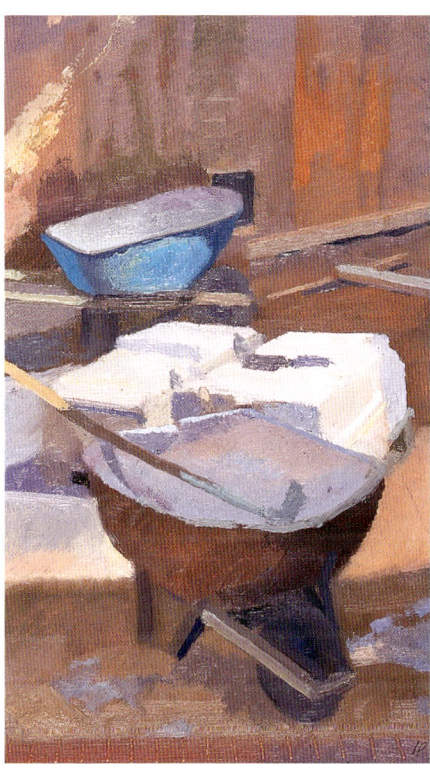

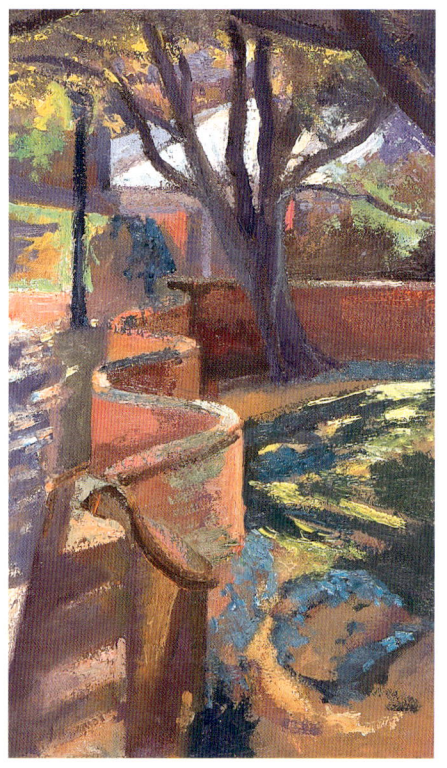 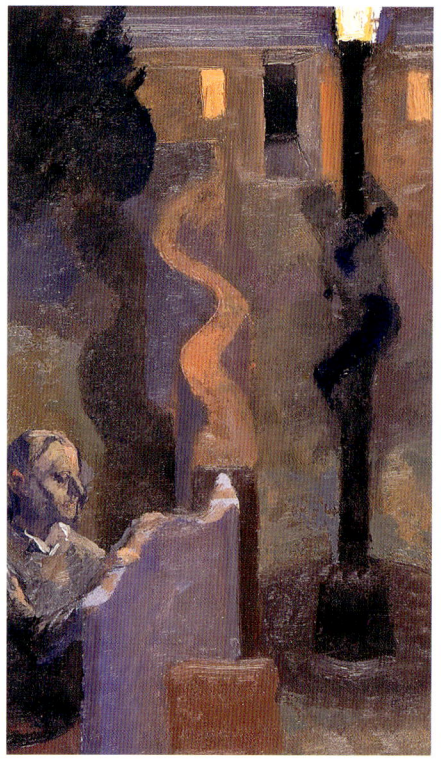 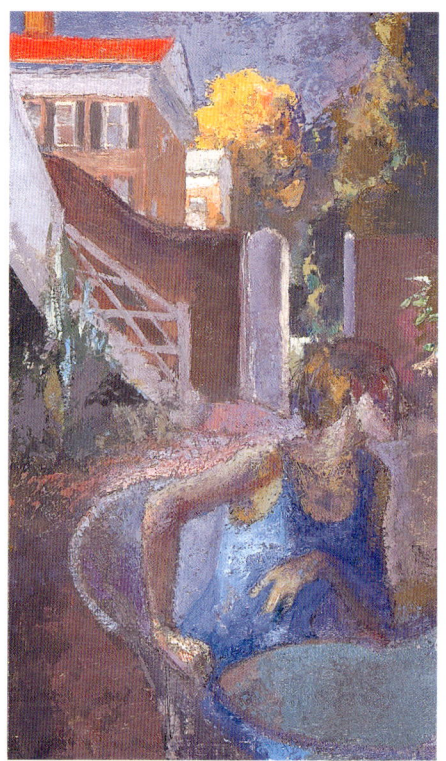

62

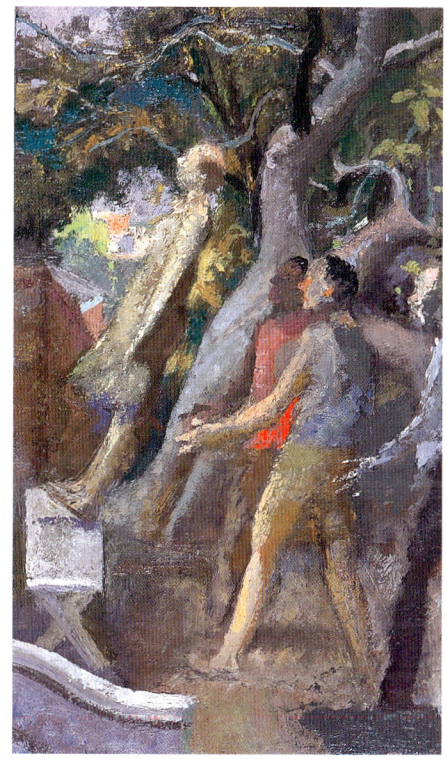 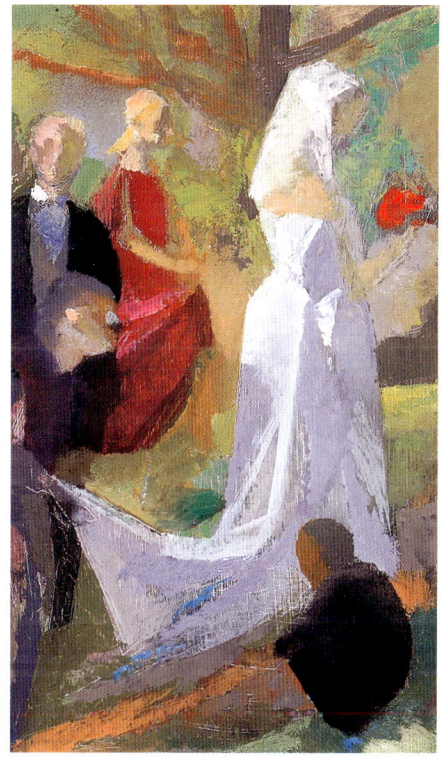 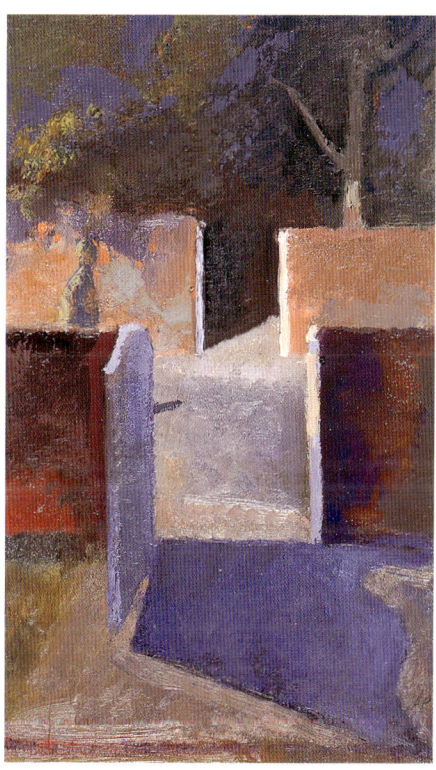

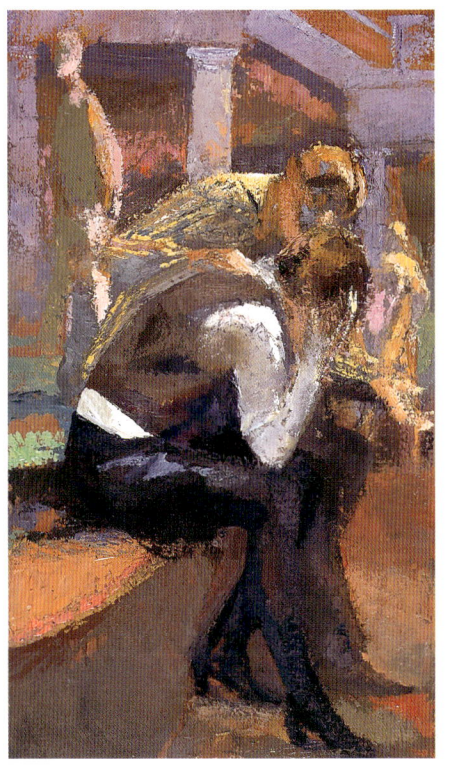 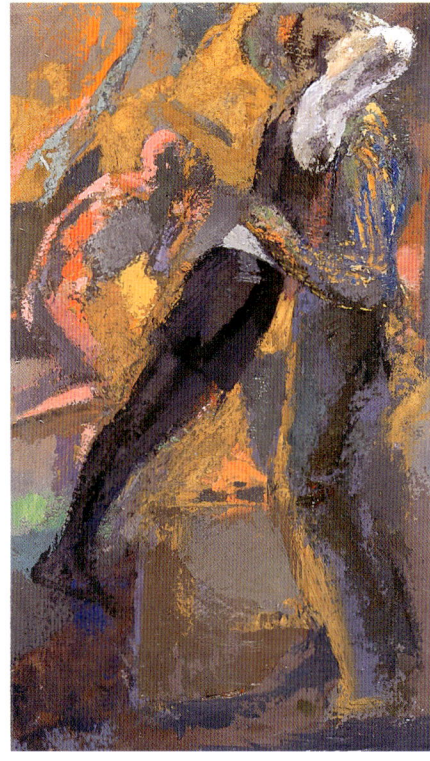 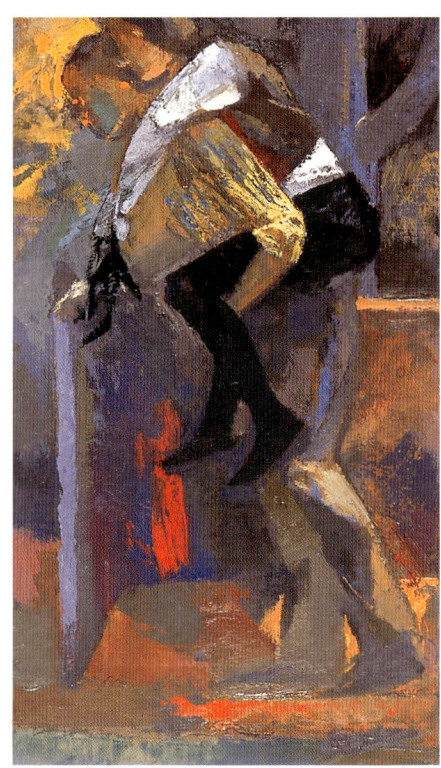

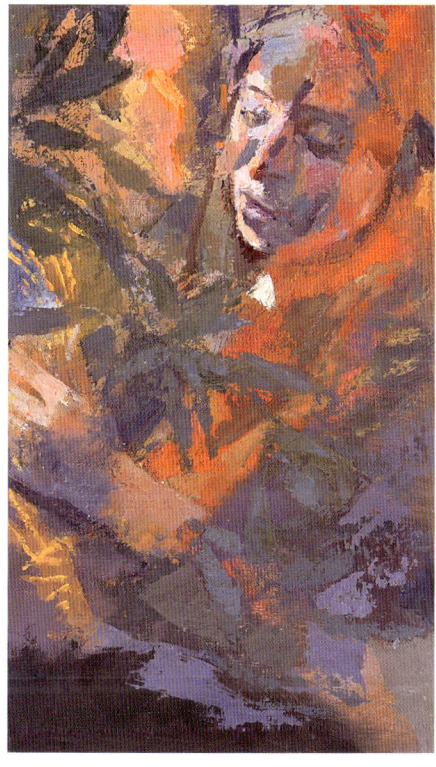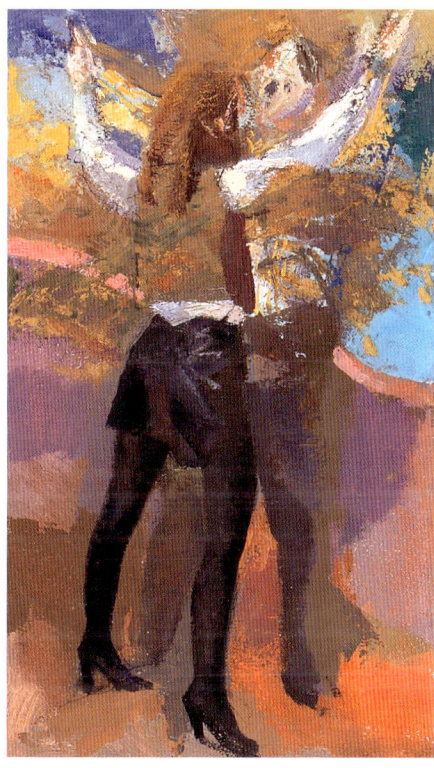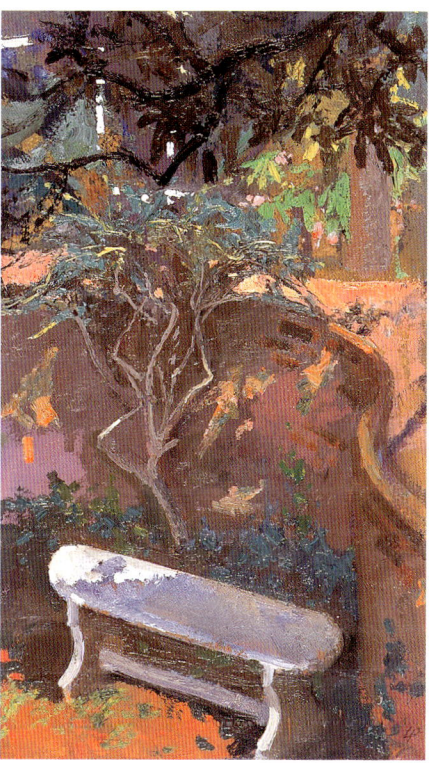

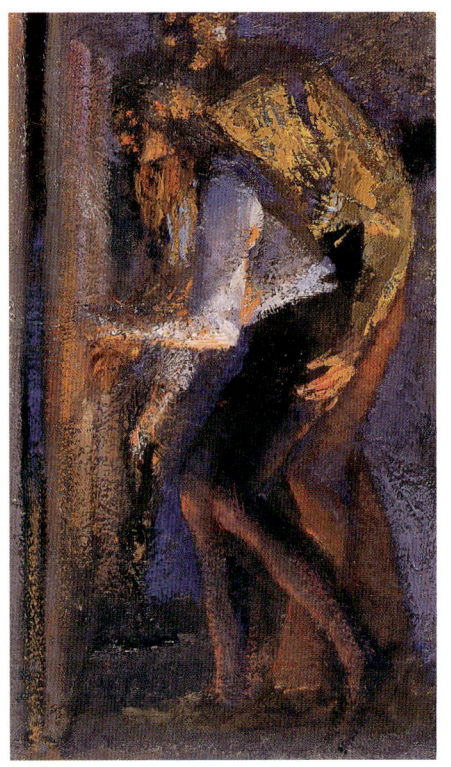 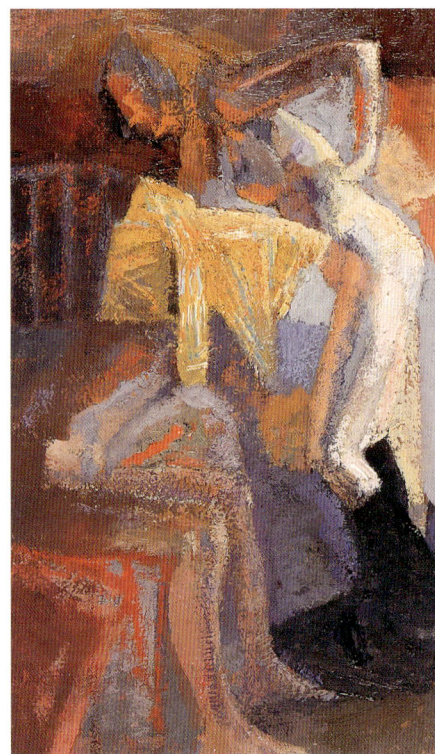 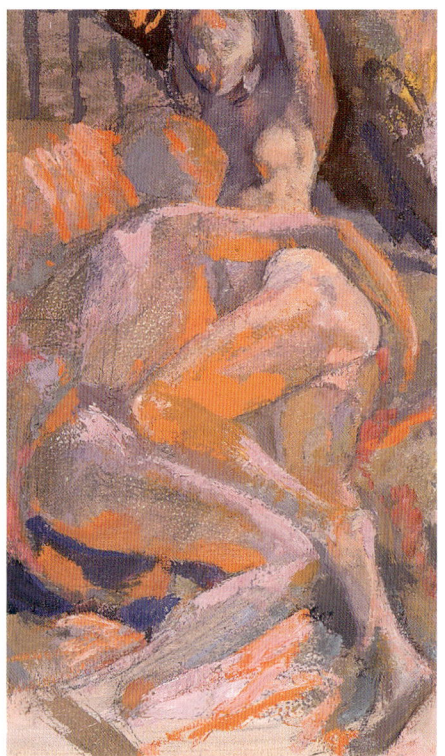

66

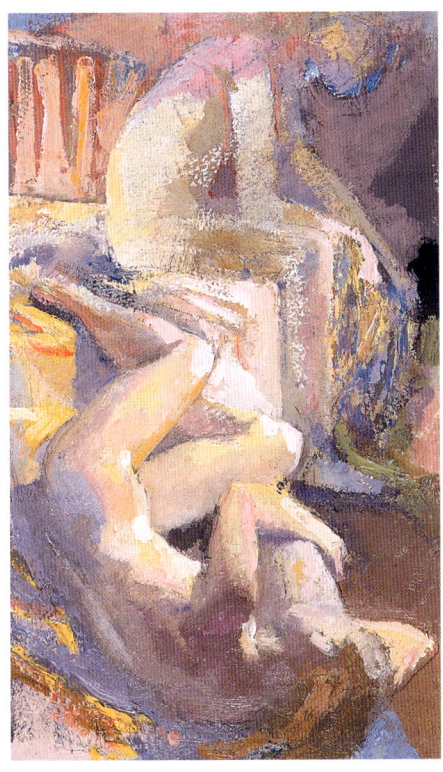
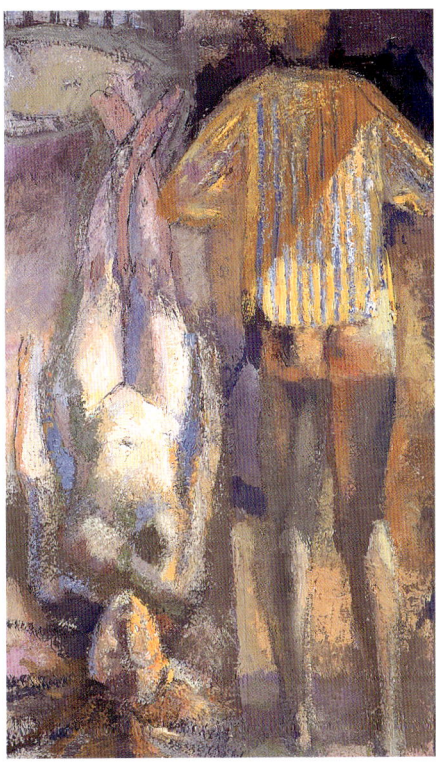
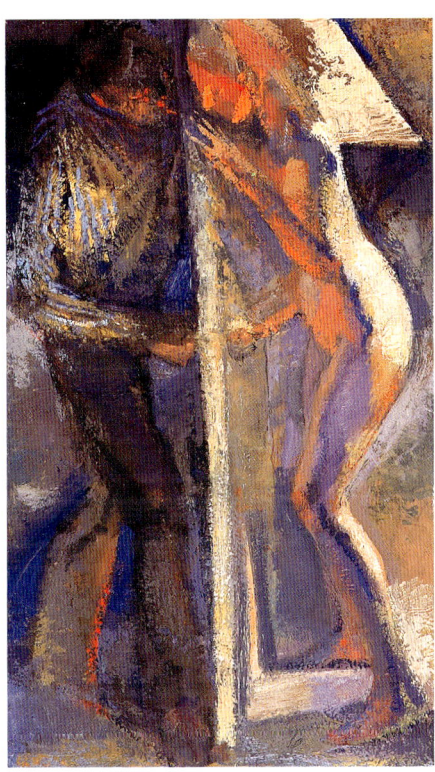

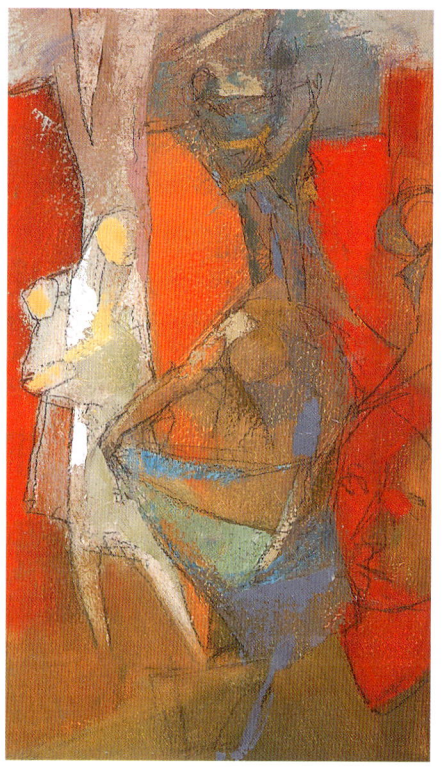 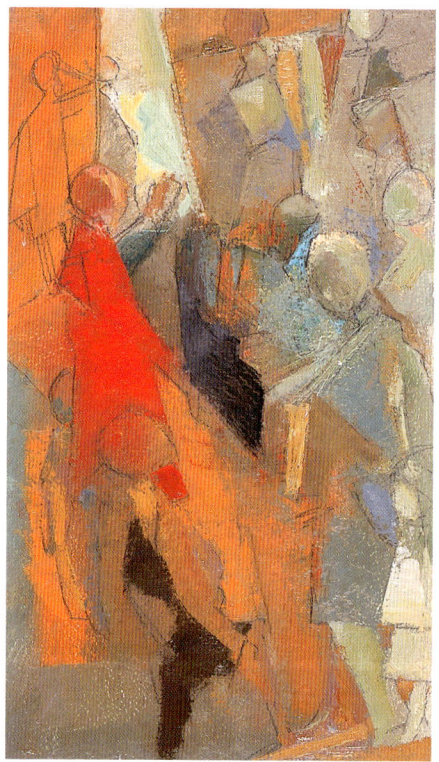 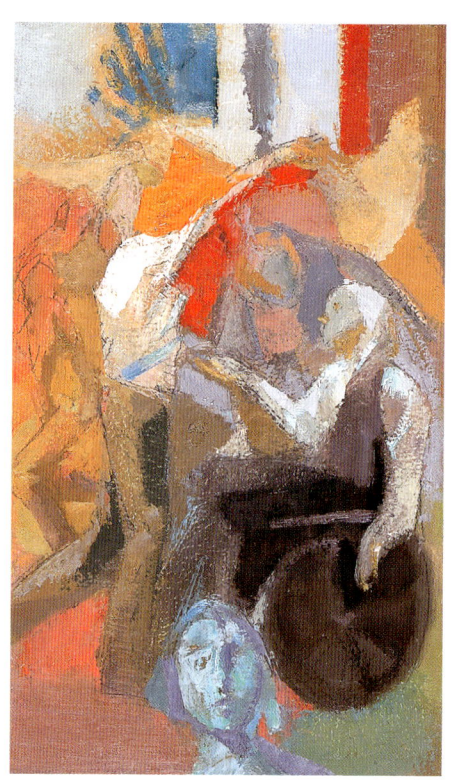

68

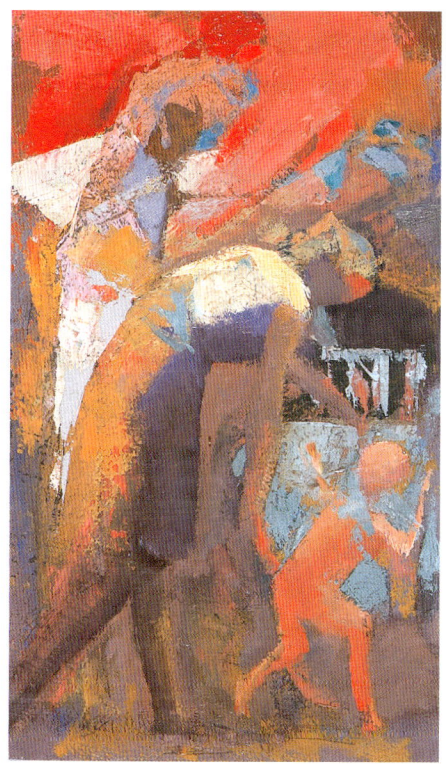 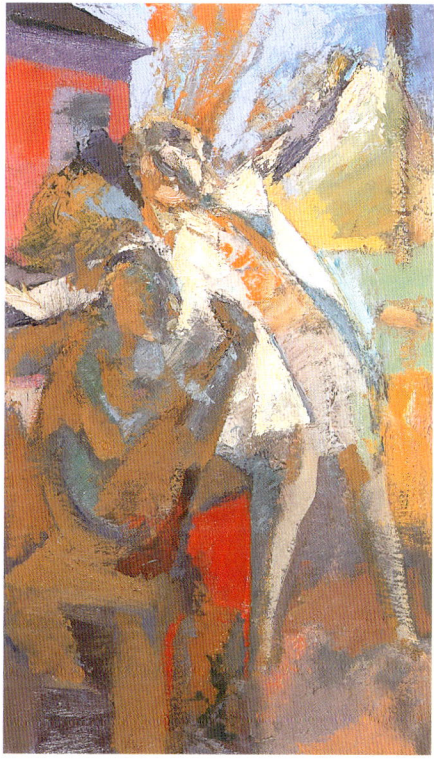 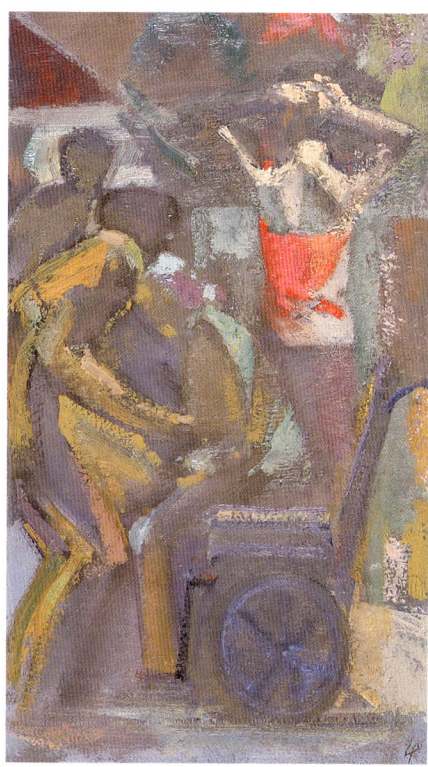

69

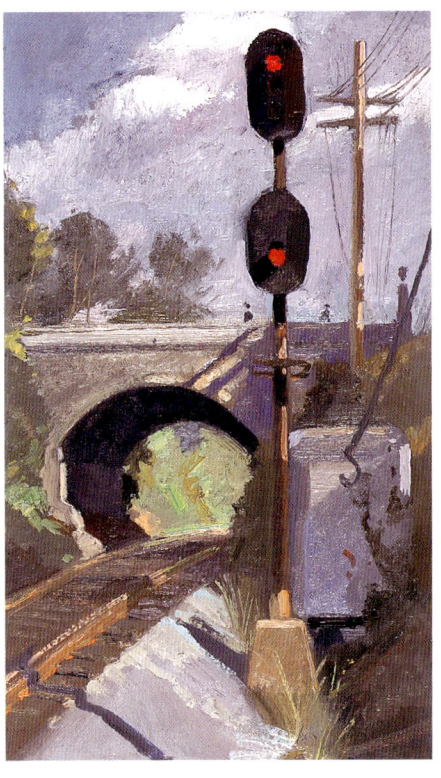 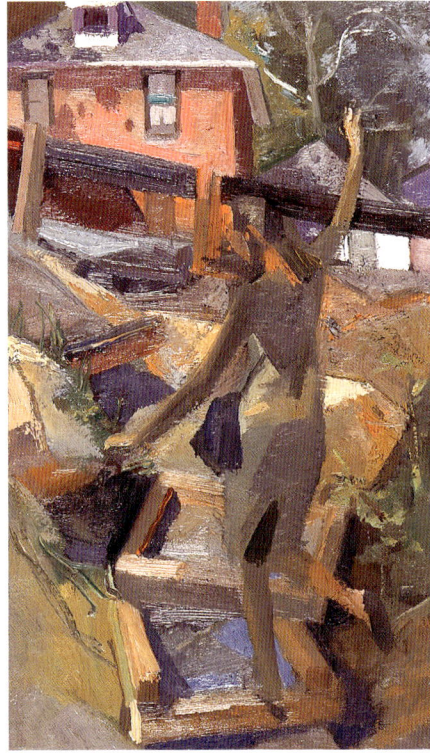 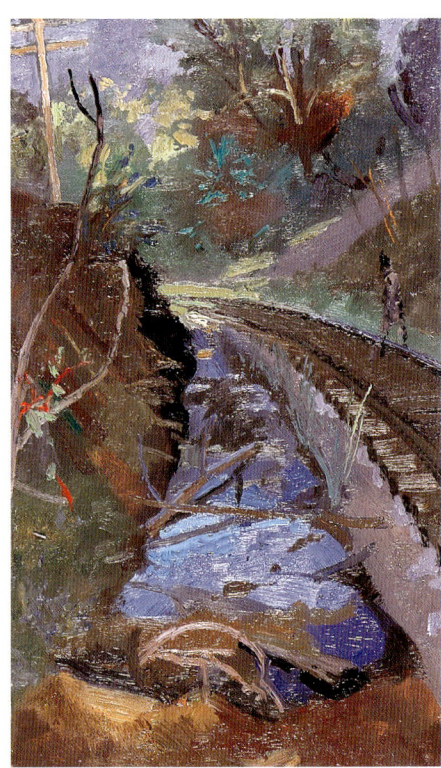

70

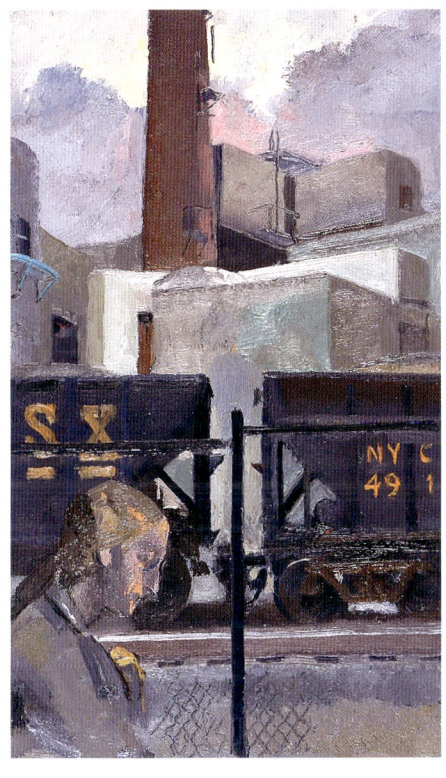 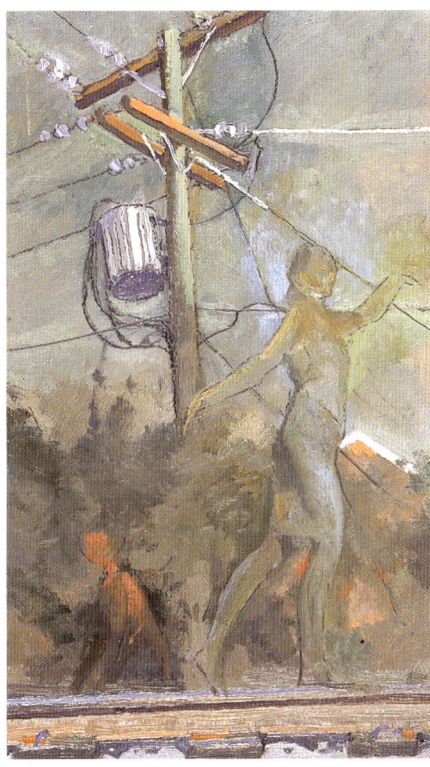 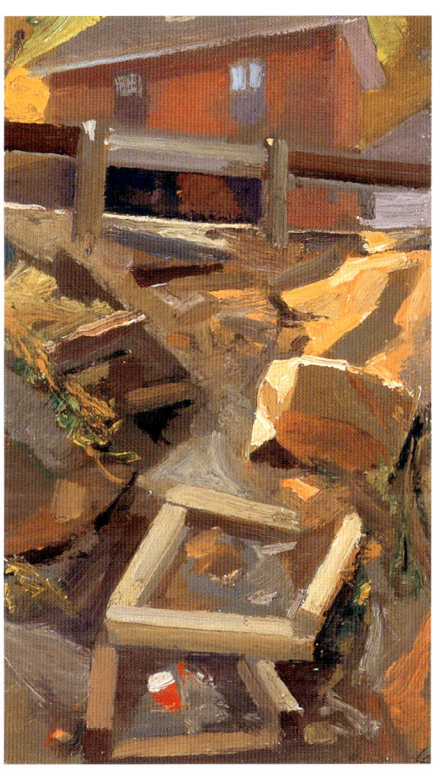

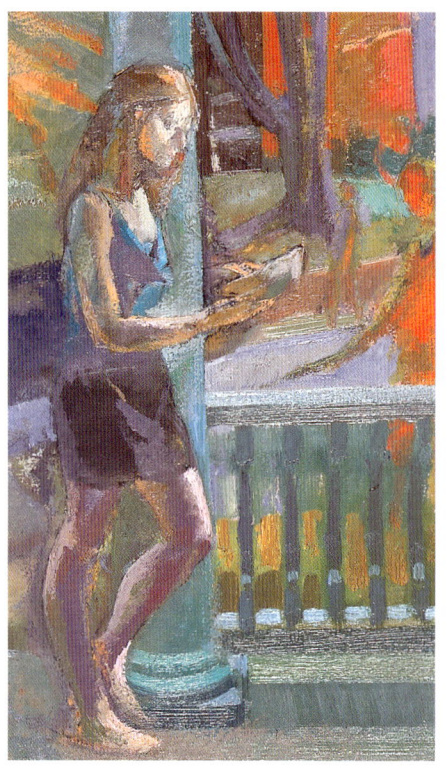 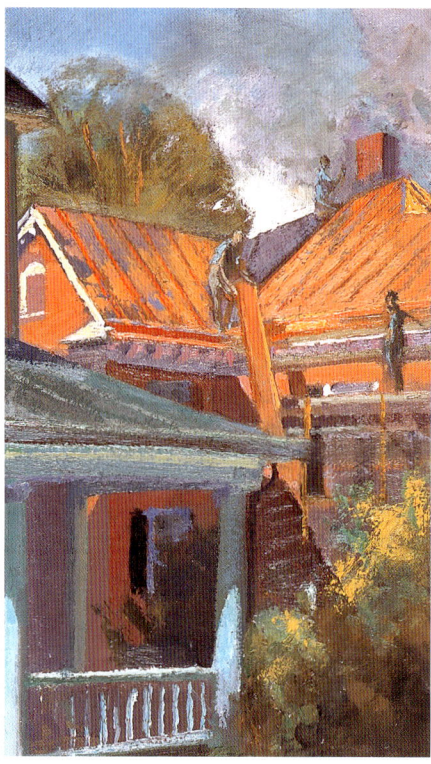 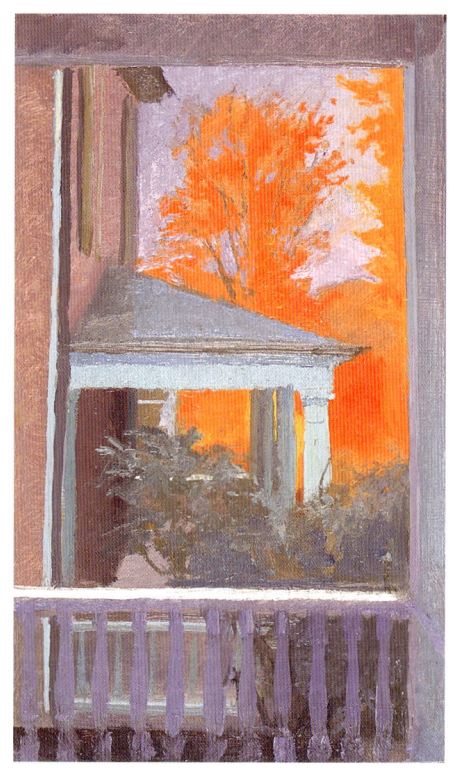

72

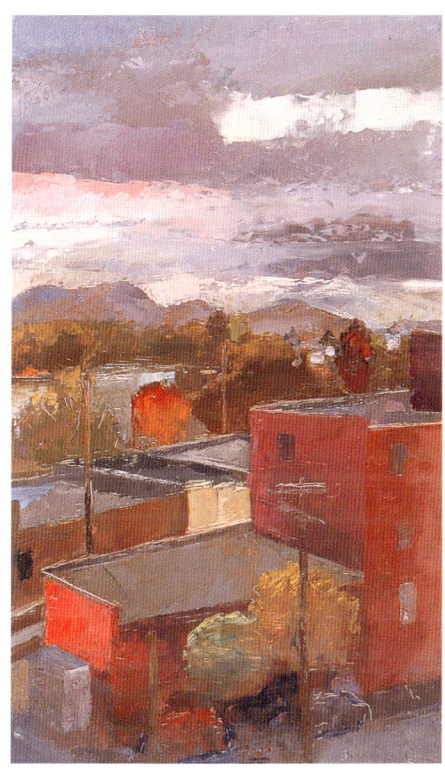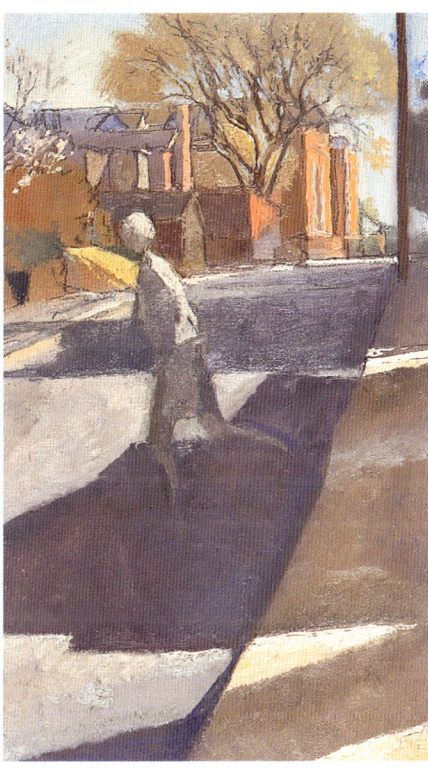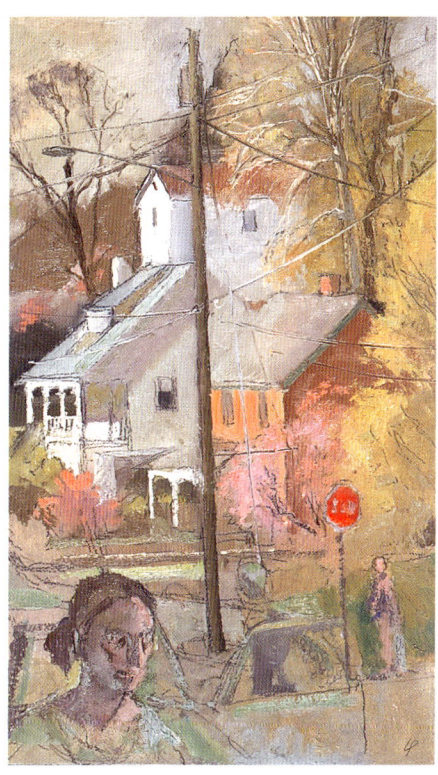

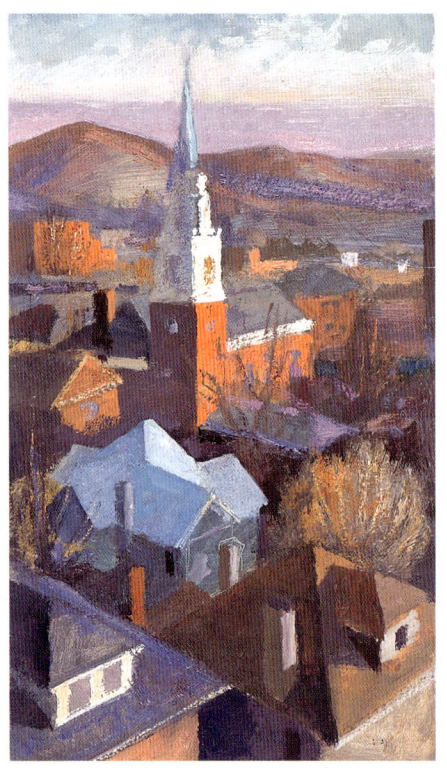 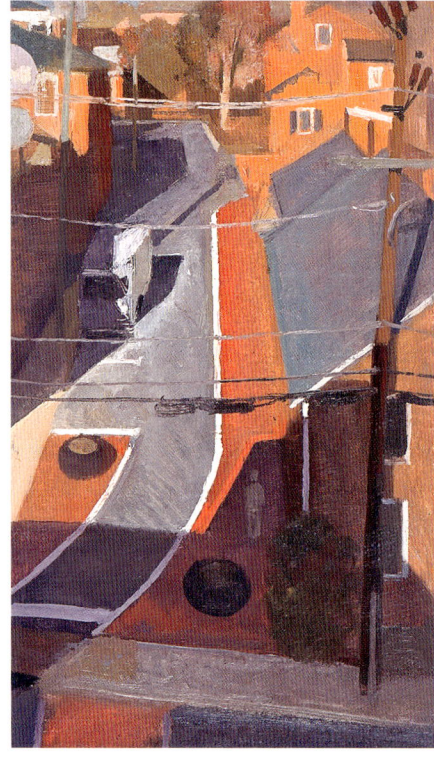 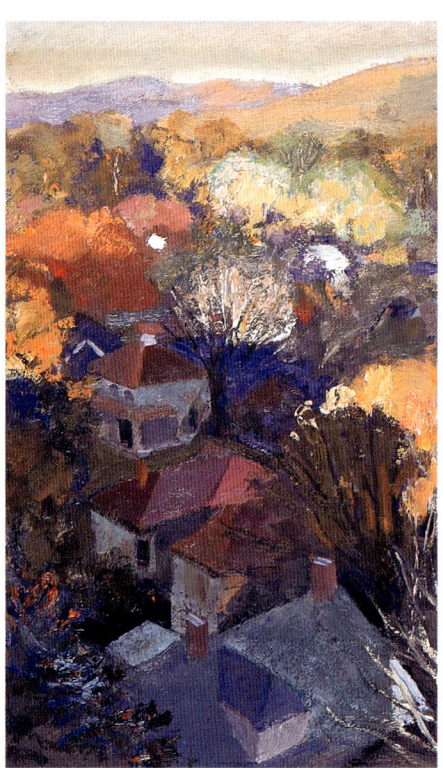

74

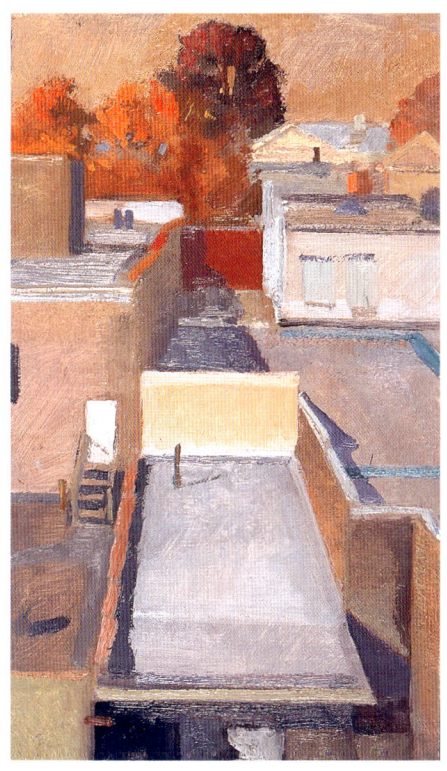 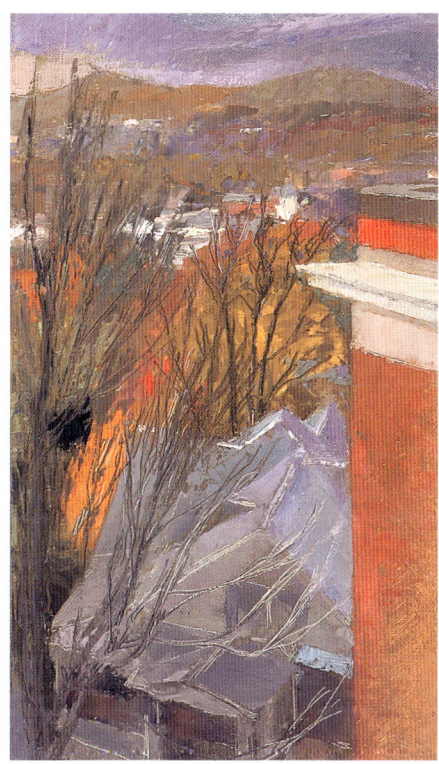 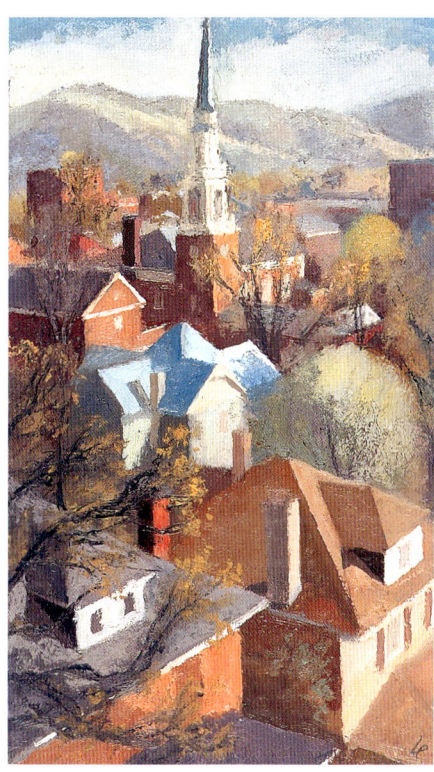

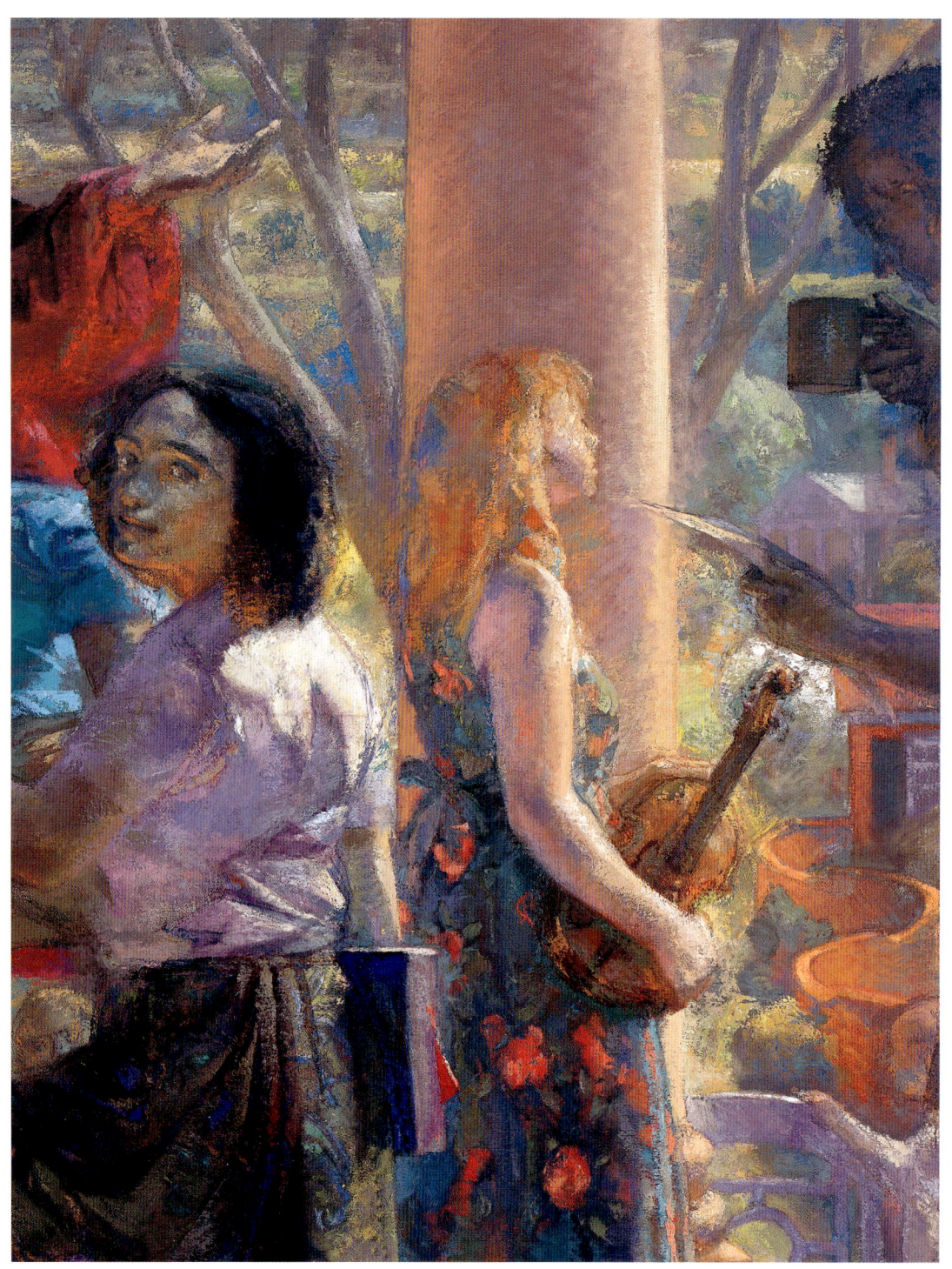

INTERVIEW WITH LINCOLN PERRY   *by Ann Beattie*

What interests you about doing large-scale murals?

I suppose the difference between paintings done on easels and murals might resemble that between the short story and the novel, or between a lyric and an epic poem, or, who knows, maybe a song and an opera. Murals have the scope, the room, to develop a story over time, to trace changes with recurring leitmotifs, to provide a sort of cumulative narrative. The problem is that we don't seem to share stories in common that the painter can take for granted and play riffs on, the way a Renaissance artist could approach the infancy of John the Baptist, say. This has been the hardest part for me, finding a narrative that already lives in the public imagination. Well, actually the hardest part is finding anyone who is aware of the option of putting a mural in a building at all. But once that particular nut is cracked, you try to find a story that resonates visually, that might mean something to the likely audience. Murals give a reassuring sense that you can connect with people, that they will see your work over and over and perhaps get something new from it each time.

How did the concept for the U.Va. mural originate?

I loved this place from the day I saw it. I loved the underlying sense of metaphor in the architecture, the feeling that Mr. Jefferson wanted students to go on a kind of secular Pilgrim's Progress, so that walking through the original campus, or Lawn, becomes educational in itself. You have to attain the knowledge stored in the Rotunda/library, go uphill to earn it, then you descend into the world at the open end of the Lawn guided by the Pavilion/classrooms, out into the mountains beyond. It seemed to me that this effort is reenacted by all students who have graduated since the school's inception, so even though the red-headed girl or protagonist is moving in a linear way across the span of Cabell's lobby, she is part of this cyclical repetition, this continuity.

Since the space where the painting would be installed already existed, were there certain restrictions or problems—or even advantages—you had to work with?

Good question. So far I've always done murals in spaces either already planned or built. I would dearly love to work with an architect, a kindred spirit, as a collaboration. I'm pretty good at anticipating what the final space will look or feel like just from plans (a friend says all painters interested in space are frustrated architects). But Cabell had been there for almost a century when I walked in, so you're collaborating with a very tangible ghost.

What might Stanford White, the architect of Cabell, have wanted; what does his lobby want? What are its implications in terms of narrative? First of all, like White himself, I'm not sure the building should even be there. It blocked off the Lawn, making its guiding arms into a closed embrace, a sort of box. Before 1898 you marched out into the landscape, the future. Now you sort of dribble out the holes in the box. That implied, to me, that the mural could suggest the view that used to be there, the one toward the mountains. That said, the repeating columns and pilasters suggest an episodic series of events, acts connected spatially but temporally separate and sequential. We read from left to right, so start with the first day of class in the big panel to the left, follow around to the central, punctuating panel that faces the main door, then have her graduate on the right.

So far all of the spaces I've worked with have suggested a story. The one in St. Louis, for MetLife, implied a circle, or cycle, a repeating day-in-the-life around the rectangular enclosed lobby. Joyce's *Ulysses* came to mind, only set with a businessman making the rounds from morning to night in recognizable St. Louis locations; Homer's lotus eaters in the morning at Soulard Market, the passage under the legs of Polyphemus as embodied by the columns of MetLife's building (I loved the fact that their logo looks like a big, octagonal eye), all the way around to evening back at his house in the suburbs. Or the one for Carr and Co. in D.C., where the lobby's convex curve suggested a story you couldn't take in all at once. If it had been concave, it would have suggested a diorama, the kind of

thing designed to make you feel you were there at Gettysburg in lower-tech times. So that and the fact that Carr's building was at 1700 Pennsylvania Avenue, two doors down from the White House, suggested a play on Alice in Wonderland. She steps through the looking glass into a tour of the White House as seen through various cross-cultural painting conventions—Indian, African, Asian—until she sees the Chinese ambassador greeting the president at the center of the forty-foot span. The Chinese delegation stands in a space defined by Asian nonconvergent orthogonals, while the U.S. president stands in a hallway purposely exaggerated in one-point perspective. As with the Cabell mural, you can't take it in all at once; you have to take it in as you go. Just like life.

What sort of note taking goes on before you start? Is this process very different, doing a multipanel, large-scale painting, or does such planning happen routinely before you begin any painting?

That question reminds me of Holly Wright's Christmas ditty describing "Lincoln, who never could paint without thinkin'." The biggish painting from last winter, the one of the back deck in Florida, was started without any sketches, any preparation, just a good feeling about the back deck. I don't know if we can do anything without thinking, or if I can, but certainly murals seventy-five feet wide aren't the place to work out problems better anticipated in sketches a few inches high. All those little line drawings eliminate dead ends and false starts. You and I are different in this; I remember how, in order to write an outline, a "bible," for a

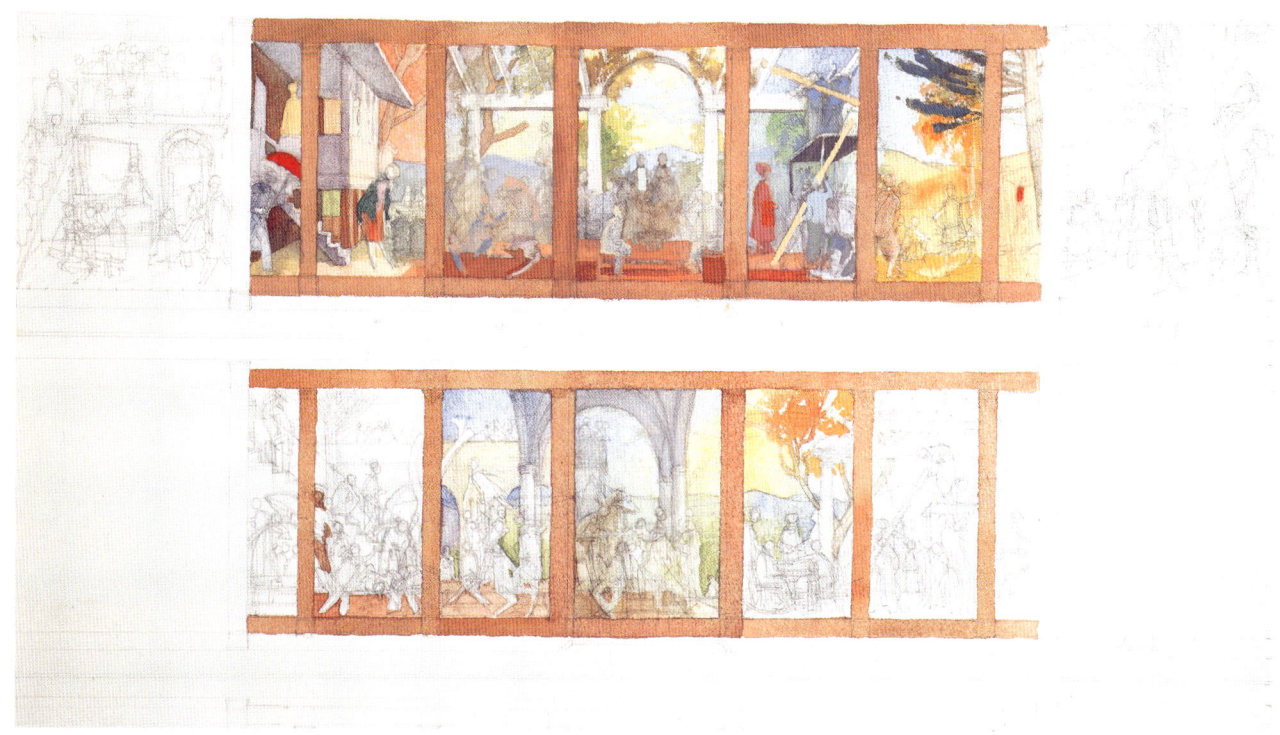

possible T.V. show, you wrote the whole thing out then condensed it. Apart from all the compositional sketches, I prowled around the campus taking notes, hoping to be surprised. Once I saw workmen rebuilding one of the Pavilion balconies, once a male cheerleader lifting a girl above his head; both made it into the painting.

If you'd had an opportunity to run your plans past Jefferson, would that have been interesting, or intimidating?

Totally intimidating.

I assume you function as both painter and critic, in the same way a writer writes and then revises and edits?

That was what we talked to the Contemporary Club of Albemarle about. You showed pages of your work, rough drafts, so blackened they looked like the censored pages my father got from the government under the Freedom of Information Act. I showed those little first drafts, the options tried and tested, that evolved into the final maquette, or sketch, ten feet across. Just as you've said novels are almost impossible to write because the mind can't hold all that information at once, unfinished murals that are just too large to hang and see together in the studio boggle the mind unless you have a pretty good mental picture of the whole.

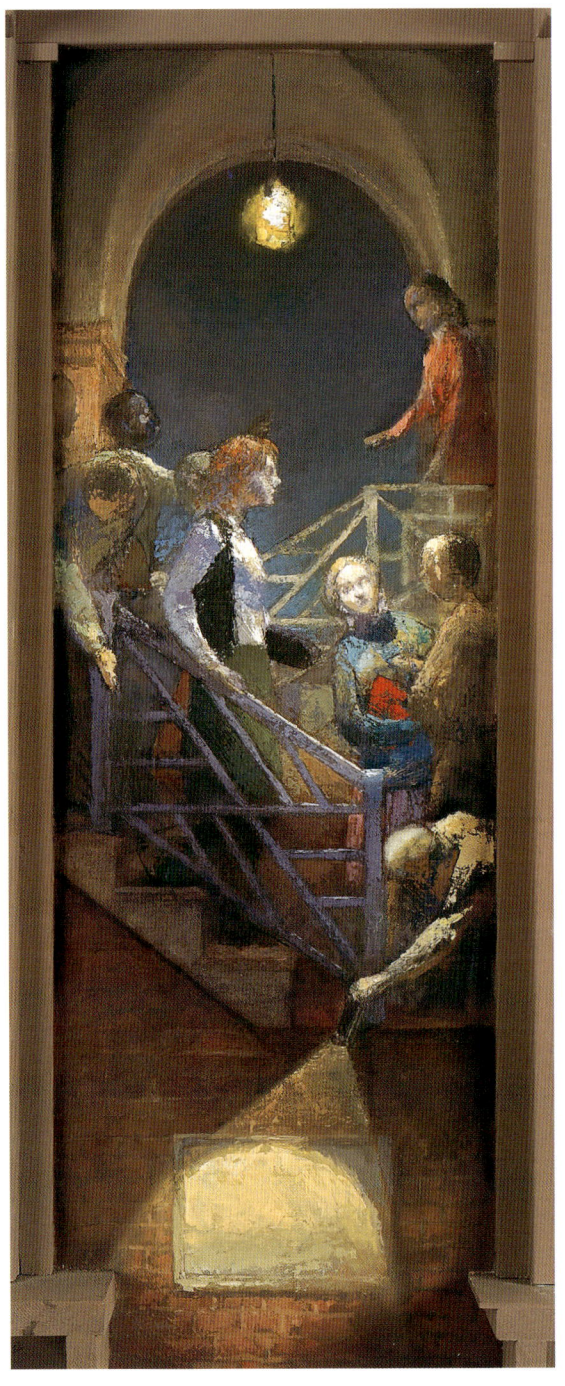

The narrative precedes the painting. Does painting the story you've worked out restrict you? Free you up, in some way?

The narrative doesn't always precede the painting. The Cabell one isn't based on an actual, borrowed text, so it evolved in response to the space. Put yourself in the red-haired girl's shoes. Big panel; first day, you climb stairs with others, work your way up a kind of spiral. Come around the corner and you're watching us descend the real stairs from your perch behind the railing. Poke your head out to see if the rain has stopped. Avoid some of the distractions or temptations of student life. The narrative evolved as a sort of two steps forward, one step back progress. She's anonymous at first, gradually coming into her own, but along the way she's rained on, teased with fast food, she sprains her ankle. She finally stands in the light; then, being a klutz, she drops her violin while being ogled by men repairing a trellis. Underlying patterns, the seasons, the times of day, those have always been important to me because I'm so troubled by our mad linear rush, our conviction that we're progressing, getting better in every way. Overall I suppose this is a somewhat optimistic narrative, because she finds her voice, her instrument, though you sense she isn't going to lead an untroubled life.

At which point did you rethink certain aspects, such as color, figure groupings, etc.?

I'm sure you remember that very bad day when I learned that redheads never wear red. That altered the whole color balance. That can happen fairly late in the process, though: the same thing happened to the Ulysses figure; his shirt went from pink to blue late in the game. The real changes are anticipated in the ten-foot-wide maquette; I tried videotaping that process, thinking it might make an informative documentary, but nothing came of it. It was a bit complicated: the middle seven panels were planned first, then money was raised for the large, flanking panels and the ones above the stairs. My first shot at the second panel made it as overpopulated as all the others, and though I like the idea [reproduced on page 80], I felt the viewer needed a rest at some point, and that the protagonist wasn't always such a social creature.

At what point do you find models, and how do they affect the process, especially if the models are people you know?

My guess is that the sequence resembles your writing, as I've observed your process. First, we seem to need to know where the stage is set, what the place feels and looks like, then we gradually populate it with characters who reveal themselves to us as we go along. The first candidates for the protagonist were in effect southern belles, the kind of perfect young lady who fascinated me when I first came to teach at U.Va. and who waltzes down the Lawn in *Jefferson Dreams*. The redheaded model I found was wonderfully awkward, which fit my sense that she would inevitably have setbacks in life, that she was a sort of everyman, or everywoman. I've drawn scores of people and only a few have had the right combination of comfort in their bodies, whether graceful or gawky, and the kind of personality that makes it companionable to spend so much time together. Sanity is a must—though I find myself often acting as unpaid therapist, hearing about their troubles. A therapist who pays the patient. When friends model, that adds a layer of meaning for me, even if most viewers won't share what might even be an in-joke. I put David Summers in the position of Plato in the central panel, knowing that he sees himself as an arch-Aristotelian. I trust he forgives me.

Most people have no idea what went on behind the scenes—how the paintings were physically done, and installed.

The timing was odd. We decided to sell our house and leave Charlottesville after living here for ten years, just as Ruth Cross and Don Innes agreed that Cabell needed a mural by me. So I did the eleven panels in Maine, on canvas, traveling back to get information I needed from the site. I didn't have enough space in my studio to do all of them at once, so I would block in two, roll them up, and return to them when the others had progressed to the same stage. I didn't see them together until I rented a warehouse. After making adjustments so they worked together, I rolled them up, rented a truck, and hired Joe Sansone, who had worked on most of my other commissions, to glue them to the walls. That was nerve-wracking, especially when the most architectural panel was glued, permanently, three-quarters of an inch too high, so none of the bricks or balcony horizontals matched. I had to repaint the bricks and balcony railing.

Barbara Walters has been made fun of for asking people what kind of tree they'd like to be. I'd be interested in the answer to that, and to hear your view on trees in general, and the landscape of the painting in particular.

I've always loved sycamores—childhood memories and whatnot—so that might be my choice. I think the most majestic, and frightening, tree I've ever seen is in our backyard in Key West: the kapok tree that could crush our house like a bug. I make fun of your parents for their fear of trees, but that one has real attitude. It's even covered with thorns. You prefer dogs to most people; I think trees are vastly underrated. They have great personality and dignity, and a tree never caused a war. In fact, Rubens ended up painting mostly landscape; you get the feeling he became increasingly disillusioned by the bad behavior he observed firsthand as a diplomat, and came to prefer nature. My whole project in art has involved painting groups of figures interacting, and I sometimes wonder if projecting these figures to the foreground doesn't inherently imply our great importance. When the government asked me to paint murals of the Mayflower Compact, the Magna Carta, etc., for the new federal courthouse in Tallahassee, I wanted to make the sea or land the protagonist, moving the action to a distance that would be analogous to our temporal distance from these events, and remind us of their place in the big picture, but they wanted humans of epic proportion.

Maybe this is an unfair question, but what would you like people to see in the paintings that might not be obvious?

When I gave a talk about the mural, someone asked if Lenin shows up in the first panel, and whether his place is taken by a cross-shaped form in the last panel—something like that. I wasn't just being cagey when I said I was glad if people brought their own interpretations to my work. I don't sign on to the fashionable idea that the viewer is the real artist, and that we, as writers or painters, don't really do the heavy lifting. You and I might not generate or control every interpretation, but I want to meet the viewer more than halfway. As I so crudely put it to J. D. O'Hara, there's a significant difference between fresh deer scat and a Vermeer. We might see the former as metaphoric, evocative, sensational, even powerful, but *The View of Delft* is a different order of experience. Maybe the latter unfolds over time, rewarding careful viewing, just as Shakespeare's work bears endless reinterpretation because there is so much there. That doesn't exactly answer your question.

What if someone is overwhelmed by the mural; how should he or she begin to take it in? (I guess this really has to do with how people view paintings in general.)

Ideally, I guess we let ourselves be carried into the work as a whole, a gestalt that precedes words. Shut up and look at the painting, as I heard a friend tell her very erudite and verbal husband at an art museum. The musician knows how to structure sound, painters should know how to structure fictive space, but that doesn't mean the listener or viewer has to be a composer to take it in. I used to think structure, space, the kind of things that go into conceiving any painting should almost advertise themselves, but when we listen to a symphony, such factors are often subliminal, clear only to prac-

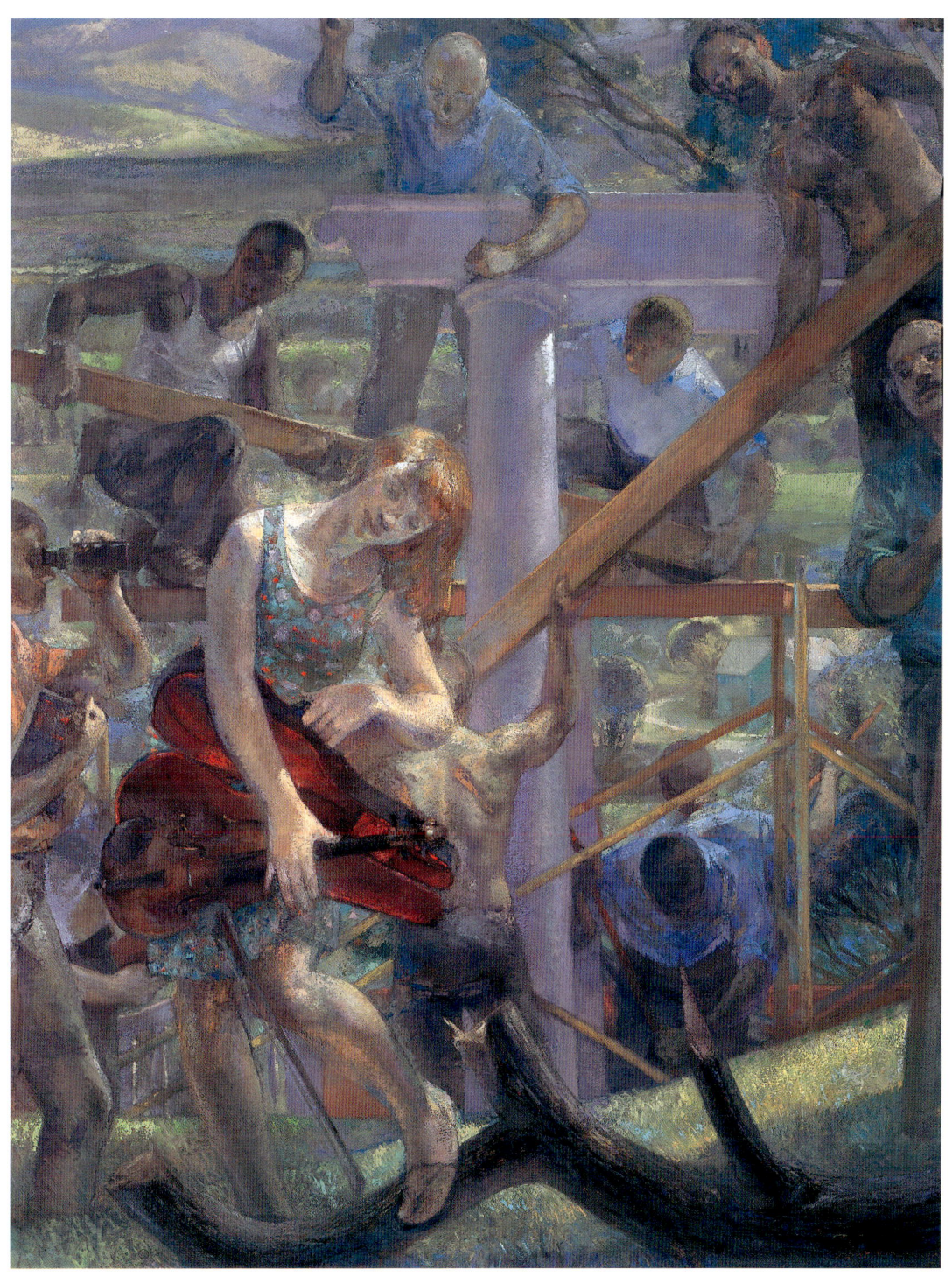

titioners. There's a modernist bias toward making the means apparent: impressionist brushstroke, cubist building blocks, etc.; but at some point a painter such as myself has to draw a line between marks that convey human character or personality and marks that draw attention to themselves as art. My teachers worked out such boundaries for themselves, always reminding us that form and content were inseparable, and they accepted that people with more hands-on experience of painting would "get" or even care about aspects of their work that others might not. But that isn't supposed to make people feel inadequate or that they're missing something. I love Shostakovich string quartets, and I'm not a musicologist. I just listen to them, over and over again. So if there are instructions built into the mural, they're visual, and probably take time, and repeated exposure, to unfold.

Are the different emotions and different reverberations in the various panels something that can be expressed more easily in a multipanel painting than on one canvas?

Absolutely. At least for me. Again, symphony versus tone poem; there's just more canvas. I've tried to imply multiple readings in lots of multipanel paintings, even fairly small ones, like the *Music of Time* series. The possibilities are immense, from the kind of clear temporal sequence you might find in Dürer's Passion prints to the witty discrepancies in Hogarth's "progress" series, which seem didactic but contain all sorts of ironic subterfuges. Just as you found in trying to write for movies at Sundance, the visual image carries entirely different freight than the spoken or written word. I don't hold with the idea that all experience is language-based, and agree with David Summers's warning that "linguistic imperialists" would have the visual be a subset of language. I don't know, maybe the relationship between the linguistic signifier and that which is signified is ultimately arbitrary, but is that really true of a painting by Caravaggio, a sculpture by Bernini? Altarpieces often used to have a saint in majesty, timeless and iconic, then below that you'd see a number of little predella panels that told the stories of the saint's miracles or martyrdom. You needed both; you wanted things brought down to earth, to somehow match the way your world felt, the messy way you knew it to be. The icon made things seem too simple, too taken care of, when you knew how various and frustrating and strange it could all be.

At some point you must have thought (those times you weren't thinking, "Tutto è sistemato!") about how your finished cycle would fit into the context of other large-scale paintings you admire. There was more than a wry game involved in alluding to things from the School of Athens *painting that exists on the flip side, so to speak.*

The Raphael copy was already there, mounted on the opposite face of the wall that holds my central panel, and I certainly play off that in terms of the poses of what I guess you could call the school of Charlottesville. It is a bit intimidating to be matched against Raphael, but that's more the way people used to think, both artists and audience. Going down the Grand Canal in Venice, you see a vast conversation. Start at St. Mark's and head up-

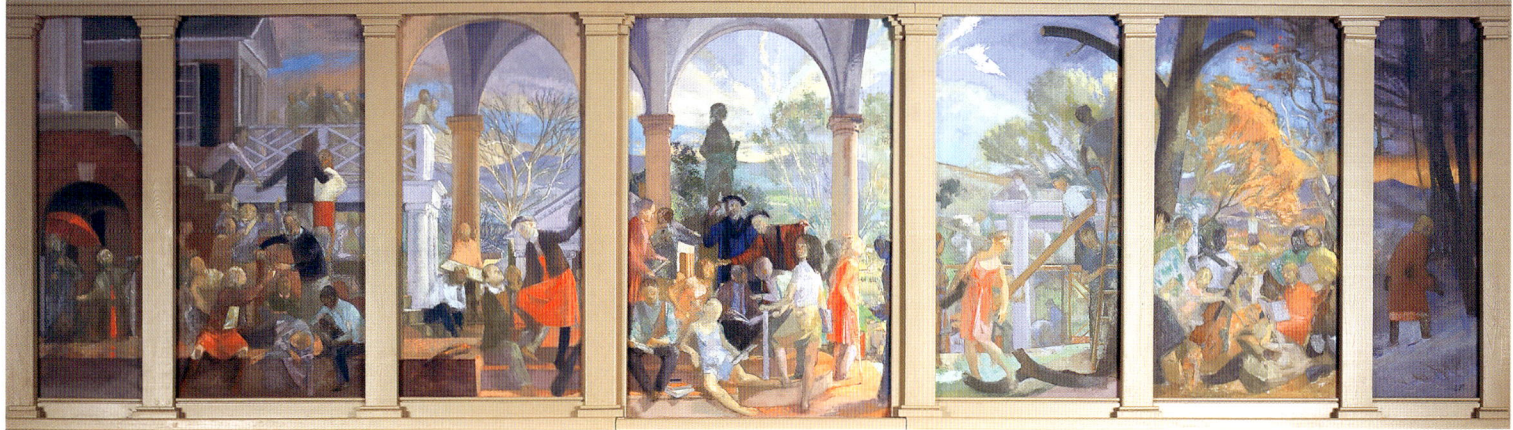

stream, and every façade responds to every other with tremendous respect, as if saying, "Yeah, I see what you did there, and how about this variation, how about unifying the windows like this, or casting even deeper shadows with a balcony?" Unfortunately, you get to the train station and this joyous conversation turns to a shouting match, with modernist buildings berating rather than complimenting the ones you've just motored past in the vaporetto. It's the collaborative conversation with the past, with artists whose work lives on, that interests me. The sheer quality of our tradition is absolutely mind-boggling. Remember Würzburg, where Tiepolo seems alive and well? He and I wouldn't share a language, but I hope we could understand what the other was doing in his work. Maybe he would have hired me to grind his paints.

Is there anything about the project that seems unfinished?

I would dearly love to paint the panels that face the first and last panels. I've even made maquettes to let ideas simmer. And, hey, I even walk up the staircases to either side of the murals and fantasize about what those walls might want: certainly images that continue the passage from culture to nature. Additional panels would make the lobby come full circle rather than remaining linear. Time's cycle versus time's arrow. Solving those kinds of problems just makes my day; I love it.

Remember how great it was to drive around in your convertible that spring night when the painting was finished, delivered, unloaded, and installation about to begin?

As I recall, I was pretty nervous about the mounting process, all the things that could (and did) go wrong, but I remember it well. The really great ride was when it was all done, when *tutto* really was *sistemato*.

List of Plates

24–25   *The Music of Time I*
2002
6: 12 x 7 in./oil on masonite
Courtesy of Les Yeux du Monde

26–27   *The Music of Time II*
2002–3
6: 12 x 7 in./oil on masonite
Collection of Alice and Dan
Malcolm

28–29   *The Music of Time III*
2002–3
6: 12 x 7 in./oil on masonite
Collection of Carol and Bill
Stevenson

30–31   *The Music of Time IV*
2002–3
6: 12 x 7 in./oil on masonite
Courtesy of Les Yeux du Monde

32–33   *The Music of Time V*
2002–3
6: 12 x 7 in./oil on masonite
Collection of Mr. and Mrs. Richard T. Spurzem

34–35   *The Music of Time VI*
2002–3
6: 12 x 7 in./oil on masonite
Private collection

36–37   *The Music of Time VII*
2002–3
6: 12 x 7 in./oil on masonite
Collection of Prue Brown and
Paul Stetzer

38–39   *The Music of Time VIII*
2002–3
6: 12 x 7 in./oil on masonite
Collection of Sarah and Douglas
DuPont

40–41   *The Music of Time IX*
2002–3
6: 12 x 7 in./oil on masonite

Collection of Charlotte and
Ralph Dammann

42–43   *The Music of Time X*
2002–3
6: 12 x 7 in./oil on masonite
Courtesy of Les Yeux du Monde

44–45   *The Music of Time XI*
2002–3
6: 12 x 7 in./oil on masonite
Courtesy of Les Yeux du Monde

46–47   *The Music of Time XII*
2002–3
6: 12 x 7 in./oil on masonite
Collection of Prue Brown and
Paul Stetzer

48–49   *The Music of Time XIII*
2002–3
6: 12 x 7 in./oil on masonite
Collection of Michael and Re-
becca Williams

50–51   *The Music of Time XIV*
2002–3
6: 12 x 7 in./oil on masonite
Courtesy of Les Yeux du Monde

52–53   *The Music of Time XV*
2002–3
6: 12 x 7 in./oil on masonite
Collection of J. and Alison
Bolen

54–55   *The Music of Time XVI*
2002–3
6: 12 x 7 in./oil on masonite
Courtesy of Les Yeux du Monde

56–57   *The Music of Time XVII*
2002–3
6: 12 x 7 in./oil on masonite
Courtesy of Les Yeux du Monde

58–59   *The Music of Time XVIII*
2002–3

6: 12 x 7 in./oil on masonite
Collection of Mr. and Mrs. Richard L. Nunley

60–61   *The Music of Time XIX*
2002–3
6: 12 x 7 in./oil on masonite
Courtesy of Les Yeux du Monde

62–63   *The Music of Time XX*
2002–3
6: 12 x 7 in./oil on masonite
Courtesy of Les Yeux du Monde

64–65   *The Music of Time XXI*
2002–3
6: 12 x 7 in./oil on masonite
Courtesy of Les Yeux du Monde

66–67   *The Music of Time XXII*
2002–3
6: 12 x 7 in./oil on masonite
Courtesy of Les Yeux du Monde

68–69   *The Music of Time XXIII*
2002–3
6: 12 x 7 in./oil on masonite
Courtesy of Les Yeux du Monde

70–71   *The Music of Time XXIV*
2002–3
6: 12 x 7 in./oil on masonite
Collection of Richard Crozier
and Marjorie Balge

72–73   *The Music of Time XXV*
2002–3
6: 12 x 7 in./oil on masonite
Courtesy of Les Yeux du Monde

74–75   *The Music of Time XXVI*
2002–3
6: 12 x 7 in./oil on masonite
Courtesy of Les Yeux du Monde

76   *The Student's Progress*, panel 6,
detail
Cabell Hall, University of Virginia

79   *The Student's Progress,* initial
      studies
      1996
      13 1/4 x 24 in./gouache
      Collection of Don and Alison
      Innes

80   *The Student's Progress,* maquette,
      panel 2
      1997
      29 1/2 x 10 in./oil on masonite
      Collection of Don and Alison
      Innes

83   *The Student's Progress,* panel 7,
      detail
      Cabell Hall, University of Vir-
      ginia

85   *The Student's Progress,* maquette,
      panels 3–9
      1997
      35 x 125 in./oil on masonite
      Private collection